The Added Dimension

Dedication

This book is dedicated to my wife Ruth whose patience and good humour has allowed me to pursue this immense task and who has helped and encouraged me throughout the past six years. I have no doubt that, without her on-going support and practical advice, my thesis and subsequent book would never have reached its final stages.

The Added Dimension

Jewish Primary Schools and Their Effect on Family Life

Dr Mervyn Leviton

ISBN: 978 1 898100 89 8

Cover design by Clare Brayshaw

Prepared and printed by:
York Publishing Services
64 Hallfield Road
Layerthorpe
York
YO31 7ZQ
Tel: 01904 431213   Website: www.yps-publishing.co.uk

Published under the auspices of the United Synagogue Agency for Jewish Education, London.

Contents

Foreword by the Chief Rabbi Sir Jonathan Sacks

Since the dawn of its collective history the Jewish people has predicated its survival on Jewish education. Its citadels were schools, its heroes teachers, and its passion learning and the life of the mind. That remains essential if Judaism is to flourish and survive.

Within British Jewry there has been a renaissance of Jewish education in recent years. Many new Jewish day schools have been built. There has been an explosion of education-based activities: formal, informal, child, adult and family. British Jewry has always been a loyal community. It now has the chance of becoming a Jewishly educated and literate community. That is a consummation devoutly to be wished.

The impact of these changes needs to be carefully researched, and that is what Dr Mervyn Leviton has done. He has asked an interesting question: what effect do Jewish primary schools have, not just on the children themselves, but their families? Does it affect their religious observance? Do better Jewishly educated children lead to more committed and practising Jewish parents? The answers he arrives at are enthralling and encouraging.

What this research reminds us – and we need reminding – is that in Judaism, education begins at home, continues at home, indeed is part of what we mean by a Jewish home. As our greatest prayer, the Shema, tells us, Torah (the text and texture of Jewish education) is a conversation between the generations. Often it is parents who teach their children. But there is a no less ancient strand that speaks of children teaching – or at least sharing their lessons with – their parents. That, as those who have experienced it know, is both a privilege and a delight. Judaism cherishes the voice of a child. Indeed a Jewish parent is one who says to his or her child, as God said to Abraham: Walk on ahead of me.

One of the most beautiful of rabbinic sayings is: 'Call them not your children but your builders.' Children are the builders of the Jewish tomorrow. Our thanks to Dr Mervyn Leviton for the fine way in which he has let us see how this is happening today.

A message from Simon Goulden BSc (Eng.)

Chief Executive of the United Synagogue Agency for Jewish Education

To those of us involved in Jewish education in the United Kingdom, it has become axiomatic that Jewish day schools are a 'good thing'. How could they not be, when the number of children attending them has grown fourfold in the last fifteen years and now the majority of Jewish children in the country, at least those in the major conurbations, receive their Jewish education at nurseries and full time day schools.

But for far too long, this belief has been just that, with no empirical evidence to back it up. Worse, there has been no evidence to show the effects of children attending Jewish day schools on their families, their home Jewish practice and observance.

Dr Mervyn Leviton is one of the most respected professionals on the Anglo-Jewish education scene today. A teacher, headteacher, mentor and guide for thousands of children over many years, his research has set out to test one of the fundamental foundations on which Jewish day schooling in Britain has been built: that the education of the children would have a direct and positive outcome on the home practice of the parents.

Through detailed and painstaking research involving 234 families, the hypotheses were tested. The results make not just for fascinating reading on the state of the Anglo-Jewish community at the start of the twenty-first century, but go to the heart of what Jewish education is all about. It will be equally of interest to educators, community leaders, planners and parents.

A message from Jonathan Faith

Chairman of the Strategic Alliance for Jewish Education

My wife Sharon and I feel privileged to have become involved in the educational work of Dr Mervyn Leviton. His painstaking and meticulous research and the revealing conclusions which flow from it, should be required reading for anyone involved with the education of Jewish children. Furthermore, his findings and conclusions should be a significant influence in how resources are directed in Jewish education from now on.

The research Dr Leviton has done is of considerable benefit to work we are doing at Strategic Alliance for Jewish Education (SAJE) and it is certainly not just a useful academic exercise. The main remit of our organisation is to assist Jewish educational organisations in fully achieving their potential in their endeavours.

The research has influenced us to direct our resources in two specific areas. Firstly, in our work to assist schools in helping them to set out a clear vision for themselves, Dr Leviton's work is a 'must-read' for those involved in the process. In particular, by having clearly set out parents' aspirations for their children's education, it would be foolhardy not to take this new information into account.

The second area is where we are directly involved in the education of parents themselves. Dr Leviton clearly demonstrates there is an appetite among parents to become more educated Jewishly at the stage of their lives when their children are at Jewish Primary School. If a method was found to teach the parents at this time, the potential benefit to their children's education would be enormous, particularly if it led to more Jewish observance in the home. Dr Leviton's work has galvanised us at SAJE to find creative methods to get these parents into the classroom. We can now be confident that this is likely to be the most opportune window to reach these families and we as a community can no longer afford to let it pass.

Acknowledgements

I wish to acknowledge my appreciation and thanks to a number of people who have played a valuable part from the inception of my research until its conclusion.

To the Chief Rabbi Sir Jonathan Sacks for his continued interest in my research and for agreeing to write the foreword to this book.

To the United Synagogue Agency for Jewish Education under whose auspices this book is published, and to its Chief Executive, Simon Goulden, for his support and encouragement.

To Dr Jo Cairns and Dr Roy Gardner, my supervisors at the Institute of Education, University of London, who guided and encouraged me throughout my research. Their patience, clarity of vision and extensive knowledge have enabled me to remain focused from the earliest days of my thesis until its conclusion.

To the headteachers, governors and parents of the three schools who agreed to participate in this research study.

To the UJIA (United Jewish Israel Appeal) and the Scopus Jewish Day School Trust (previously Zionist Federation Educational Trust) for their financial support towards the costs of undertaking this research.

To Duncan Beal, Amanda Hancock and Clare Brayshaw of York Publishing Services and Glynis Harris for their practical advice and guidance throughout all the publishing stages to bring this book to fruition.

Finally, to Jonathan and Sharon Faith whose generosity and total commitment to the cause of Jewish education have made possible the publication of this book.

Introduction

An examination of the historical and social background of the Jewish community in the UK during the 20th century shows that there had been a gradual but clear weakening of Jewish religious observance. The previous Chief Rabbi, Lord Jakobovits, was rightly convinced that only the strengthening of Jewish education amongst the youth would stem the increasing tide of assimilation in Britain. More Jewish schools were needed to reinvigorate Anglo-Jewish religious life. His plan to change this somewhat gloomy scenario was detailed in his 1971 work *Let My People Know*, published under the auspices of the Jewish Educational Development Trust.

However, evidence from substantial research in the USA shows that this alone was not necessarily the solution. Most studies have generally focused on the later effects of a Jewish day school education on the pupils themselves and have examined the extent of their adult Jewish communal and religious identification. The evidence showed that it was only when the parents and their home life had supported the religious ethos and the teaching in the school that their children continued to identify in later years with Jewish religious life. Conversely it has also been shown that when parents had not supported the school's religious ethos and practice at home, there was little likelihood of their children leading a religiously observant life in later years. Further details of these research studies may be found in the Bibliography section at the end of this book.

I believe that if it can be shown that Jewish day schools do have an influence on the religious practice of the parents, it would suggest that these pupils will be more likely to continue to identify with Judaism in their adult years in a more practical and positive Jewish religious manner.

Chapter 1

The background to this research

Some Jews are born into a religious family,
Some acquire religion,
Some have religion thrust upon them.
(with apologies to Shakespeare)

So what makes a Jewish person become more religious and more observant? Of course there are many valid answers to this question. It could be the influence of more religious friends. It could be due to being inspired by the Rabbi's sermon. (I know it sounds unlikely but it might happen.) It could be due to personal involvement in an emotional–religious experience, such as the birth of a child, or marriage to a more religious spouse, or sadly due to bereavement.

But there is another reason why many previously less or non-observant Jews are becoming more religiously observant in their Jewish lives. I believe that, with many families, it is due to the direct or indirect consequence of sending their children to a Jewish primary school. I have been both a teacher and a headteacher at Jewish day schools in London during the past thirty five years and have frequently heard comments such as:

'This school has definitely made parents more religious. I know of families who never kept anything, but since they sent their children to a Jewish primary school they go to synagogue on a Shabbat and now buy only kosher food.'

There is a frequently voiced assumption amongst those involved in Jewish education that less observant or non-observant parents whose children attend a Jewish primary school, have increased their own level of religious observance due to the influence of their children and the school. But in fact no previous research in this area has been carried out in the United Kingdom.

With the current demand of many Jewish parents wanting to send their children to Jewish schools, I felt that the time was right to test this assumption in a thorough manner. I chose to do this by means of both questionnaires and in-depth interviews with parents of pupils attending three Jewish primary schools in England.

The research was conducted in two Jewish primary schools in London and one in the north of England. For reasons of confidentiality they have been given fictitious names:

Rubin Jewish Primary School in London

Norton Jewish Primary School in London

Brook Jewish Primary School in the North of England.

A total of 234 families participated in this research.

Each school had a minority of families who admitted to being either very observant or totally non-observant. The religious observance of the majority of the families varied at different levels between the above two extremes. It is of interest to note from a recent report of the Institute for Jewish Policy Research, *The Future of Jewish Schooling in the United Kingdom,* that 'half of all Jewish day school pupils are from non-Sabbath-observant homes'.

My main aim was to determine whether or not there had been any noticeable change in the level of religious observance and practice of the less or non-observant parents which directly or indirectly could be attributed to the influence of their children and the Jewish primary school they attend. All the families confirmed that at no time did they anticipate that there would be any change to their own level of religious observance due to their children attending a Jewish day school.

I decided to focus on primary schools rather than secondary schools for a specific reason. At a primary school there is a greater opportunity for parental contact on a more regular and intimate basis with the school, as most of the parents generally live near to the school. Secondary school pupils, however, tend to travel longer distances to school and parental contact with these schools is generally restricted to school presentations or to parents' evenings in order to discuss their children's academic progress. Of course, there may well be many examples of parents who have increased their level of religious observance due to the influence of their children attending Jewish nursery schools or secondary schools.

I did not approach the more 'right-wing' religious schools as it is most likely that the parents of these pupils are already very observant and would expect the school to support their home values and traditions. It is of far greater value to examine the effects of what may be termed 'middle of the road' or 'Central Orthodox' schools which are more likely to have a reasonably large number of Jewish children from less or non-observant families.

As the data would incorporate many in-depth interviews with families, it was unrealistic to work with more than three schools. It was important therefore to select three different types of Jewish primary school. All three schools have pupils from both Ashkenaz (European) and Sephardi (Spanish/Portuguese and Middle Eastern) backgrounds.

Rubin is a two-form-entry voluntary aided school in North-West London, in an area which has a large and vibrant Jewish population.

Brook is also a two-form-entry voluntary aided school but it is in a provincial town in the North of England in an area where the Jewish population is slowly decreasing. It was useful to compare the similarities and differences between Jewish schools in London and the provinces.

Norton is a small private school in London. In a similar manner, I felt that it was important to compare the attitudes, views and behaviour of these parents who have chosen the private sector when compared with the other two state schools.

The religious background of the parents

Although all the parents of pupils at all three schools are Jewish, they are likely to be members of one of four various differing religious groups which are termed:

Orthodox, Masorti/Traditional, Reform/Progressive and Liberal/ Progressive.

Religious observance and practice common to all four groups may be loosely defined as carrying out or participating in any action which is a part of Jewish religious law, custom or tradition. It may also be understood as not carrying out any action proscribed by Jewish religious law, custom or tradition.

When investigating the families whose level of religious observance had increased, I have not differentiated between these four groups. There may well be members of the Reform or Liberal synagogues whose level of religious observance and practice is higher than that of some families who are members of an Orthodox synagogue. Nor, for the purpose of this research, have I differentiated between each group's understanding of who can be regarded as 'Jewish'.

I have investigated the reasons for any increase in religious observance but have not compared one family with another. There are families whose starting point of previous religious practice was low or non-existent. There are others whose initial level of religious observance was higher. In both sets of cases, however, there may have been instances of an increase of religious observance of the parents which have been attributed by them to the influence of their children and to the school.

Bearing this in mind, it will be shown that some families, for example, may previously never have observed the Pesach dietary laws but are now doing so. Other families may never have kindled Chanukah lights but are now doing so. Some may have attended synagogues only rarely but now attend more frequently. Some may have regularly attended synagogue on the Sabbath but are now observing other Shabbat laws which previously had not been observed.

These are only a few examples of the types of families whose level of religious observance has increased and been attributed to the influence of their children and the school. It is therefore of little importance to which synagogue or religious group they are affiliated. The main thrust of this research was to determine if the children and the school were in any way responsible for stimulating any such increase in religious observance and practice among their parents.

Why this research does not include areas of faith and belief

It is more difficult to measure, in an accurate and reliable way, any changes in a person's level of religious belief. It is far easier to measure a quantifiable change in religious practice. Bearing in mind that the majority of the laws of Judaism are of a practical rather than a philosophical nature, I feel that research into what a Jew does and how a Jew behaves is, for the purpose of this study, of greater importance and relevance than what a Jew believes.

Of course there is no doubt that faith and belief play a major role in all areas of Judaism. There have been many Rabbinical scholars who have listed and explained the main and specific areas of Jewish faith. The most famous and generally accepted Orthodox scholar in this connection is Maimonides (1135–1204) whose Thirteen Principles of Jewish Faith remain the prime foundation of the essence of Orthodox Jewish belief.

Although both belief and practice are fundamental to Judaism, as to all religions, it is the 'practice' of Judaism that is examined in this book. This concept of action and practice has been emphasised from the time of Moses when the Israelites were about to receive not only the Ten Commandments but also the entire Torah (Law):

> 'And Moses came and called for the elders of the people and set before them all these words which the Lord commanded him. And all the people answered together and said, "All that the Lord has spoken we will do."' (Exodus 19: 7–8).

Chapter 2

The purpose of the questionnaires and interviews

Even in this modern world of CCTV cameras which seem to follow our every movement outside our homes, we have not reached the distasteful depths of the Orwellian concept of Big Brother watching and recording our private and personal lives in our own homes. The nature of this research obviously precluded any direct observation into the personal, private and varied activities in the lives of the families. Any research of this nature, no matter how thorough and vigorous it may be, relies entirely on the personal responses of the families to the questionnaires and interviews.

The purpose of the questionnaire was threefold:

- To obtain factual information relating to respondents' backgrounds and family history.

- To obtain data relating to measurable levels of various aspects of Jewish practice. Measurable in this sense referred to self-evaluation scores on a Likert scale.

- To identify families who would later be interviewed in greater depth in order to investigate the changes in attitudes and practice which have come about due to the direct or indirect influence of their children and the school.

Every one of the 234 families had indicated through the questionnaire that due to the influence of their children and the school, their overall level of religious observance had, to a lesser or greater degree, increased during the time that their children were at a Jewish primary school.

At all times I was fully aware that any research relying purely on data from questionnaires and interviews, and not from direct observation, is invariably open to an element of doubt about its accuracy and veracity. In his excellent work on the technique for constructing questions for interviews and questionnaires, William Foddy (1993) emphasised that 'the relationship between what respondents say they do and what they actually do is not always very strong'.

This potential problem was constantly on my mind, not only when analysing the data from the returned questionnaires, but even more so when conducting the in-depth interviews with families. I must confess that the specific factor that concerned me the most was the possible unwillingness of husbands and wives to admit to certain attitudes or behaviour. I felt that certain respondents might find some of the questions potentially threatening and might not wish to admit publicly to a specific attitude, belief or norm of behaviour.

There is no reliable way through a questionnaire or interview that one can convince respondents that total openness and honesty is essential and will be treated with complete confidentiality and that it is also crucial to the ultimate effective analysis of the data. There was always the possibility that the above problems might occur in some of the questionnaire responses that I received. Nevertheless, I feel that in the majority of cases the quantitative data illustrated reasonably accurate trends in changes of parental levels of observance. During the in-depth interviews I was able to clarify certain responses and hopefully removed any such misunderstandings and ambiguities.

A copy of the initial letter and the questionnaire sent to the parents who participated in this research is included on the following pages.

May 1998

Dear Parents,

I am writing to ask for your personal help with a doctoral research project to examine the effect of Jewish primary schools on the religious beliefs, attitudes and practice of parents whose children attend such schools. The Headteacher and Governors of your school have agreed to be included in this project which includes three Jewish primary schools.

I would be very grateful if you will be able to spend about half an hour in order to answer, <u>in total confidentiality</u>, the 15 questions on the enclosed questionnaire. Your response, together with those of other families, will help me to produce a research report which will give a clear indication of the effect of a Jewish primary school on family life. It will be a valuable guide in developing our schools in the future.

All the information you complete will be treated with the highest degree of confidentiality and there is no way that your family will be identified. However, it would be of immense value if you would also agree to be interviewed in an entirely private and confidential manner at a mutually convenient time and place. If you are willing to help further with a research interview, please write your name and address and telephone number in the section at the end of the questionnaire. If you do not wish to be interviewed leave that section blank and return the completed questionnaire anonymously.

This questionnaire should be sealed in the envelope provided and returned to the school. The envelope will be opened only by myself, and the specific personal information will not be divulged to any other person in a way that might identify your own family. If you are willing to help, please return the completed questionnaire to the school office within the next two weeks.

Thank you in anticipation of your help.

THE EFFECT ON A FAMILY OF A JEWISH DAY SCHOOL EDUCATION

(1) Please state the country of birth of the following people:

Husband..

Wife ....

Husband's parents (Mother)............................ (Father)................................

Wife's parents   (Mother)............................ (Father)................................

(2) What Jewish education did you have when you were both of school age? (Place a tick in the appropriate column)

	Husband	Wife
None	....	....
Cheder (part-time classes)	....	....
Jewish Nursery School	....	....
Jewish Primary School	....	....
Jewish Secondary School	....	....
Other (give details below)	....	....

....

(3) If either or both attended only part-time classes (Cheder) state how many times a week you each attended. Tick the appropriate sections.

	Husband	Wife
Sundays only	....	....
Sunday and one weekday session	....	....
Sunday and two or more weekday sessions	....	....
No Cheder attendance	....	....

(4) What is the level of your religious observance today in each of the areas listed below? Please give a rating from 5 to 1 and circle the appropriate number:

5 = Very observant
4 = Reasonably observant
3 = Varied
2 = Generally non-observant
1 = Totally non-observant

[a] Dietary laws at home: (e.g. Buying only kosher meat and other kosher foods and separating milk and meat dishes)

Husband	5	4	3	2	1
Wife	5	4	3	2	1

[b] Dietary laws away from home:

Husband	5	4	3	2	1
Wife	5	4	3	2	1

[c] Shabbat candles always lit:

Husband	5	4	3	2	1
Wife	5	4	3	2	1

[d] Friday night Kiddush recited at home:

Husband	5	4	3	2	1
Wife	5	4	3	2	1

[e] Shabbat synagogue attendance:

Husband	5	4	3	2	1
Wife	5	4	3	2	1

[f] Making Havdalah when Shabbat goes out:

Husband	5	4	3	2	1
Wife	5	4	3	2	1

[g] During the whole Passover week, eating only food that is kosher for Pesach:

Husband	5	4	3	2	1
Wife	5	4	3	2	1

[h] Participating in a full seder evening:

Husband	5	4	3	2	1
Wife	5	4	3	2	1

[i] Pesach/Shavuot/Sukkot synagogue attendance:

Husband	5	4	3	2	1
Wife	5	4	3	2	1

[j] Lighting a menorah at Chanukah:

Husband	5	4	3	2	1
Wife	5	4	3	2	1

(k) Did you have a sukkah at home?

Husband: YES / NO   Wife: YES / NO

(l) Any other comments you wish to add (optional).

(5) When you were adult but before you were married what was your level of religious observance? Use the same rating system as in question 4 above.

[a] Dietary laws at home:

Husband	5	4	3	2	1
Wife	5	4	3	2	1

[b] Dietary laws away from home:

Husband	5	4	3	2	1
Wife	5	4	3	2	1

[c] Shabbat candles always lit:

Husband	5	4	3	2	1
Wife	5	4	3	2	1

[d] Friday night Kiddush recited at home:

Husband	5	4	3	2	1
Wife	5	4	3	2	1

[e] Shabbat synagogue attendance:

Husband	5	4	3	2	1
Wife	5	4	3	2	1

[f] Making Havdalah when Shabbat goes out:

Husband	5	4	3	2	1
Wife	5	4	3	2	1

[g] During the whole Passover week, eating only food that is kosher for Pesach:

Husband	5	4	3	2	1
Wife	5	4	3	2	1

[h] Participating in a full seder evening:

Husband	5	4	3	2	1
Wife	5	4	3	2	1

[i] Pesach/Shavuot/Sukkot synagogue attendance:

Husband	5	4	3	2	1
Wife	5	4	3	2	1

[j] Lighting a menorah at Chanukah:

Husband	5	4	3	2	1
Wife	5	4	3	2	1

[k] Do you have a sukkah at home?   YES / NO

[l] Any other comments you wish to add (optional).

(6) How religiously observant, in the majority of the above areas, were your own parents when you were children? Circle zero if unknown. Give a rating from 5 to 0 and circle the appropriate number for each parent.

5 = Very observant
4 = Reasonably observant
3 = Varied
2 = Generally non-observant
1 = Totally non-observant
0 = Unknown

Husband's parents:	5	4	3	2	1	0
Wife's parents:	5	4	3	2	1	0

Any other comments you wish to add (optional).

(7) If possible state how religiously observant were your grandparents. Use the same rating system as above. Circle zero if unknown.

Husband's mother's parents	5	4	3	2	1	0
Husband's father's parents	5	4	3	2	1	0
Wife's mother's parents	5	4	3	2	1	0
Wife's father's parents	5	4	3	2	1	0

Any other comments you wish to add (optional).

(8) Give the sex, age and other details of each of your children and indicate with YES or NO if he/she also attended a Jewish nursery school.

	M or F	Age now	Date of birth	Age when joining a Jewish primary school	Nursery State Y or N
Child 1	....	....	....	....	....
2	....	....	....	....	....
3	....	....	....	....	....
4	....	....	....	....	....
5	....	....	....	....	....

(9) If any of your levels in question 4 were higher than those in question 5 it means that during the time you have been a parent of a child/children at a Jewish day school there has been an <u>increase</u> in the level of religious observance of either husband or wife or both. If this is so, which of the areas listed below could have played a part?

If there has been no increase in your level of religious observance during the time you have been a parent of a child/children at a Jewish day school, leave this section blank and <u>go on to question 10.</u>

Give a rating from 5 to 1 and circle the appropriate number.
5 = Maximum influence   4 = Partial influence
3 = Possible influence   2 = Minor influence
1 = Absolutely no influence

[a] Children's friendships:

5   4   3   2   1

[b] Adult friendships made through the school:

5   4   3   2   1

[c] Wishing to support ethos of school:

5   4   3   2   1

[d] Children need help with Jewish Studies homework:

5   4   3   2   1

[e] Children ask to go to Children's Services at the synagogue:

5   4   3   2   1

[f] Witnessing school assemblies and events of a religious nature:

5   4   3   2   1

[g] Children's religious activity at home, e.g. making Kiddush/participating in seder etc:

5   4   3   2   1

[h] Comments made by children at home about festivals, synagogue etc:

5   4   3   2   1

[i] Greater awareness of Israel due to school activities:

5   4   3   2   1

[j] Children are learning to speak Ivrit:

5   4   3   2   1

[k] Adult Education courses at school:

5   4   3   2   1

[l] Any other comments you wish to add (optional):

(10) <u>Complete this section only if you have left the previous question blank.</u>

There has been no increase or change in the level of our religious observance whilst our child/children has/have attended primary school for the following reasons (Tick the appropriate response(s)):

[a] We have always been an orthodox/observant family and our standards have not changed. ☐

[b] We have always observed some aspects of Judaism and our levels of observance have not changed. ☐

[c] We are a non-observant family and we do not wish to change our lives. ☐

[d] We do not feel that there is any connection between our child's education at school and our own level of religious observance. ☐

[e] Any other comments you wish to add (optional).

(11) How important were the following reasons when you chose to send your child/children to a Jewish day school? Give a rating from 5 to 1 and circle the appropriate number for each of the reasons given below.

5 = Very important
4 = Quite important
3 = A possible but not essential reason
2 = Not a priority
1 = Totally unimportant
0 = Not applicable

[a] To give our child/children the Jewish education that we (or one of us) never received.

5   4   3   2   1   0

[b] One or both of us attended Jewish day schools and we want our child/children to benefit in the same way.

5   4   3   2   1   0

[c] We are observant and the school will help to support the ethos and style of life at home.

5   4   3   2   1   0

[d] We want our child/children to have mainly Jewish friends.

5   4   3   2   1   0

[e] We want our child/children to read Hebrew and follow a synagogue service.

5   4   3   2   1   0

[f] We want our child/children to learn to speak Ivrit.

5   4   3   2   1   0

[g] We did not wish to send our child/children to other local LEA schools for the following reasons:

(i) We were concerned that our child/children might suffer discrimination.

5   4   3   2   1   0

(ii) We did not want him/her to learn about other religions.

5   4   3   2   1   0

(iii) We did not want him/her to participate in other religions and their practices.

5   4   3   2   1   0

[h] Any other comments you wish to add (optional).

(12) How important do you rate a Jewish secondary school education for your children? Circle around the appropriate number below:

5 = Very important
4 = Quite important
3 = A possible but not essential reason
2 = Not a priority
1 = Totally unimportant

Any other comments you wish to add (optional).

The next three questions ask you to give your personal views and opinions about specific statements. In each case you are requested to place a tick or to circle the view or opinion which reflects your own.

(13) Parents of children of primary school age should 'direct' their children's religious beliefs by example and practice and not encourage their children to make up their own minds as to the extent of religious observance they wish to follow.

FULLY AGREE

PARTIALLY AGREE

UNDECIDED

GENERALLY DISAGREE

TOTALLY DISAGREE

Any other comments you wish to add (optional).

(14) If a child is to benefit from Religious Education, it is important that the home reflects the values and ethos of the school.

FULLY AGREE

PARTIALLY AGREE

UNDECIDED

GENERALLY DISAGREE

TOTALLY DISAGREE

Any other comments you wish to add (optional).

(15) If your child wanted the family to become more religious due to what had been taught at school, tick which of the following would be your response:

(i) We feel that we are already leading a religious life and do not feel the need to make any change.

(ii) Totally agree for the whole family to change its lifestyle and lead a more religiously observant life.

(iii) We would be prepared to discuss a compromise with our child and perhaps change part of our family lifestyle.

(iv) We would allow our child to be more observant but not if it affects other members of the family.

(v) We are not a religiously observant family and we are not willing to make any changes to our lifestyle.

Any other comments you wish to add (optional).

IMPORTANT – PLEASE READ THIS FINAL SECTION WITH CARE.

You do not need to state your name and address on this questionnaire. However, the object of this research is to understand whether our Jewish day schools contribute to the Jewish commitment of the families of the pupils.

It would be of <u>immense value</u> if you would agree to be interviewed in an entirely confidential manner at a mutually convenient time and place. <u>If you are willing to help</u> with this important research, please write your name, address and telephone number below. Thank you for the time you have given to completing this questionnaire.

<u>If you do not wish to be interviewed, leave this section blank.</u>

This questionnaire should be sealed in the envelope provided and returned to your child's primary school. The sealed envelopes will be collected by the researcher.

JEWISH EDUCATION RESEARCH

We are willing to be interviewed

Name ....

Address ....

....

....

Telephone No...

Understanding the rationale behind the questionnaire

Question 1 requests the country of birth of both husband and wife and also of the parents of the husband and wife, i.e. the grandparents of the children at the primary school. It is possible that as a result of analysing the data received, a pattern could emerge which correlates attitudes and religious practice with specific countries of origin. This question can also be related and compared to the responses to questions 6 and 7 below, which provide an indication of the religious environment of the husband and wife when they were children.

Questions 2 and 3 relate to the type of Jewish education received by the parents when they were children. This would enable me to ascertain the relationship between parents' early Jewish education and their current levels of Jewish religious observance.

Questions 4 and 5 refer to the level of religious observance both currently and before marriage in eleven separate and specific areas relating to private and public practice. These are focused mainly on dietary laws and Sabbath and festival observance. The reason for focusing on these specific areas is to highlight any link with similar educational activities of the children at their school. These are developed in far greater depth during interviews with parents, when further examples of additional Jewish religious practice are investigated.

Questions 4 and 5 contain a number of sections that are clear and unambiguous such as whether Shabbat candles or a Chanukah menorah are always lit at the appropriate times. There are, however, some questions where the interpretation of the respondent could vary. For example 'participating in a full seder evening' on Pesach could mean different things for different respondents. What does a full seder evening mean? To some it might mean 'a family get-together' with minimum selections from the Haggadah combined with partaking of wine and matzah. To others it might mean a deep religious experience with all the rituals and explanations covered in depth.

Questions 6 and 7 are intended to elucidate an indication of the religious environment of the husband and wife when they were children. At the same time, information is requested about the grandparents of the husband and wife. The purpose of these questions is to find a possible correlation between present-day observance and previous family background. This is linked with questions 1 to 3 above.

The purpose of **question 8** is to determine how many years each child has been a pupil at the school. It is possible that this too may have some connection with the effect on parental Jewish identification.

Questions 9 and 10 are of great importance in this study. Question 9 invites respondents to comment on the reasons for any increase in religious observance during the time their children have been pupils at the school. Question 10 was included as there was the possibility, as shown in question 9, that there had not been any positive increase in the level of religious observance of either husband or wife. If this were the case, it needed an extra question to analyse the possible reasons for this. Respondents would therefore be asked to answer either question 9 or question 10.

Question 11 focuses on the reasons why a Jewish primary school was selected whereas **Question 12** lists the level of importance placed on a Jewish secondary school education. The responses to these questions were intended to give a clearer indication of the broader and deeper values and attitudes of the parents.

Finally, **questions 13, 14 and 15** explore the attitudes and opinions of the parents in three main areas: [a] the role of parents in 'directing' their children's religious beliefs: [b] the importance of the home in reflecting the ethos and values of the school: [c] parental attitude towards a child who requested greater Jewish religious identification of the family.

The selection of families to be interviewed

I did not include those parents who were already observant before their children started attending the primary school. It was evident that in all those families the religious ethos of the school reflected their own religious attitude and behaviour. In fact, in a few cases, the families were living in an even more religiously observant manner than that advocated by the school.

These parents might have become observant due to many other factors such as marrying a more observant partner, or coming under the influence of more observant friends or the Rabbi of their synagogue. It was also possible that couples had previously decided to raise any future children in a religiously observant manner. To investigate such reasons would certainly be a valid and valuable research study, but it would come outside the specific area of my own aims for this research, namely to study the effects of the school on parental religious observance.

I am aware that no data is available on parents who declined to complete a questionnaire or to be interviewed. This is, of course, not an uncommon factor in many other research studies. I make no claim that the findings of this research will have relevance for all or the majority of less observant parents whose children attend a Jewish primary school. What the data will strive to illustrate will be the effect of a Jewish school on the lives of those who agreed to participate. Nevertheless it is reasonably clear from a survey of the backgrounds of the parents who responded to the questionnaire that they appear to come from a reasonable cross-section of families.

A brief outline of the content and purpose of the interviews

The aim of the interviews was to focus on and develop key areas of the questionnaire responses. The interviews were of a semi-structured nature with ample opportunity for the interviewees to discuss their thoughts and opinions in a relaxed and non-threatening environment. Wherever possible, husbands and wives were interviewed together and encouraged to give their own personal and combined thoughts on the specific topics being discussed. Each interview, lasting about one and a half to two hours, took place in the privacy and comfort of the family home. A request to tape the interview was agreed by every interviewee and an assurance of total confidentiality was given to each family.

The basic interview questions are summarised below:

- Tell me about your early life as a child and teenager. In which way were you and your parents involved in any Jewish religious life?

- What were your views about your level of religious observance when you were first married? What did you decide to do or not to do?

- What were the reasons that made you decide to send your child/children to a Jewish primary school?

- What other primary school options were there for you to choose from? What were your reasons for not considering any of these options as a primary school for your child/children?

- What do you feel are the positive points about a Jewish primary school?

- Do you feel there are any negative points about a Jewish primary school?

- You indicated in the questionnaire that over the last few years your level of religious observance has increased. What have been the main reasons for this?

- To what extent do you feel that the school has acted as a catalyst in being initially and primarily responsible for these changes in your life?

- Do you feel that your lives would have been different if your child/children had not attended a Jewish primary school? Give some examples if possible.

- To what extent has your child/children been a key factor or influence on your religious behaviour? Can you give me some examples?

- Can you give any examples of occasions when your child/children wanted to demonstrate an aspect of Jewish life which had been learned at school?

- What are your thoughts and feelings when you listen to them. What effect does this have on you?

- Has your child/children been an influence on the family in respect of Sabbath observance? Give some examples.

- What would you say are your main reasons or your main driving force for going to shul on Shabbat? Do you think that you would have attended so frequently if it were not for your child/children?

- To what extent do you attend synagogue on Pesach, Shavuot and Sukkot? Is it because of your child/children that you attend on these festivals? Give examples and reasons.

- How difficult is it for you to take time off from work to attend the Synagogue on Pesach, Shavuot and Sukkot if they fall on weekdays?

- If your child was unable to attend synagogue on such a festival, would you still take off time from work to attend?

- Have you ever purchased a lulav and etrog for Sukkot? To what extent was this due to requests from your child/children?

- What would you say are the main reasons that have brought about an increase in your observance of the Jewish dietary laws? In which way might your child/children have played a part in this decision?

- How important is it for a family to support the religious and Jewish ethos of a Jewish primary school? What were your reasons? What do you feel is the religious ethos of the school?

- Have you been influenced by attending school assemblies and events of a religious nature? Give some examples.

- Is it possible that your children's friendships with other children may have been a factor causing a change in your own religious life-style? Give some reasons and examples.

- Is it possible that adult friendships made through the school have caused a change in your own religious life-style? If so, give some examples.

- Have there been any other influences apart from the school which have made you move to a more religiously observant life?

- Have you experienced any problems in changing your life-style? How have your friends and wider family reacted to this? How have you coped with the pressures of less observant friends and family who would like you to join in with them as before?

- Do you think that parents of children of primary school age should 'direct' their children's religious beliefs by example and practice and not encourage their children to make up their own minds as to the extent of religious observance they wish to follow? What are your thoughts about this idea?

- What are your feelings and thoughts about the future for yourselves and your children? How might you react if your teenage child/children rebelled and did not wish to observe Shabbat or kashrut?

- Looking further ahead to the future, what would be your response to an adult son or daughter who wished to marry out?

- What would you do if your child wanted the family to become more religious due to what had been taught at school?

- What would be your response if your child wanted to behave in a religious manner when not at school? For example a boy who wants to wear his kippa and tsitsit when he was not at school, when at home, when out and on holiday.

- Is there any conflict between the religious life of yourselves and your children?

- Is there any conflict between the religious life of yourselves, your children and the grandparents of the children?

- Do you think that the religious life of your family is being driven by both of you or is one of you the main driving force?

- What do you foresee as your own level of observance in the future as the children get older and begin to live their own lives? Do you think you will maintain this life style?

All of the interviewees were relaxed and fully prepared to answer my questions with openness and frankness. I did not sense any embarrassment amongst the families interviewed. It was also clear that on many occasions there was a difference of opinion between husband and wife that helped to establish a greater sense of veracity to their responses. As with all semi-structured interviews, I was fully prepared and willing to follow a new line of questioning where necessary in order to delve more deeply into the significance of a specific comment.

Chapter 3

Early childhood experiences of the parents

The questionnaire responses showed that there were very few parents who had not received any formal Jewish education at all during their childhood years. Approximately half of the parents in my survey had received their Jewish education purely at part-time cheder centres, usually on synagogue premises on a Sunday morning. The other 50% had attended Jewish primary schools. It was interesting to note that some 40% of the parents had also attended a Jewish secondary school.

The number of parents who had attended Jewish nursery schools was relatively low (approximately 30%) when compared to the far higher percentage of children who attend Jewish nurseries today. A report by the IJPR (2003) estimates that over 22,000 children are currently attending Jewish pre-school nurseries.

The purpose of this category of questions was to determine whether or not there is any correlation between the childhood experiences of the parents and any later increase in their level of religious observance. In the responses to the questionnaire there were ten main areas of the childhood experiences of parents which appear to have been the foundation for increased religious observance in later years.

1. Their own parents were observant.
2. Being part of a close and cohesive family.
3. Attending a Jewish primary/secondary school.
4. The problem of being perceived as 'different' at a non-Jewish school.

5. Their Jewish identity was retained through the influence of growing up in a strong Jewish community.
6. Participating in Jewish youth groups.
7. The effect of the Holocaust on their own family.
8. Involvement in Zionism and Israel studies.
9. Bereavement as a factor in religious observance.
10. Influence of marrying a more observant spouse.

However, I also found that there were four examples of childhood experiences which created a negative attitude towards later adult religious practice.

1. The rejection of an Orthodox family upbringing.
2. A secular family upbringing.
3. The influence of non-religious friends.
4. The influence of marrying a non-observant spouse.

I was interested in exploring the childhood experiences of the parents during the interviews to determine whether or not the various pressures and demands from their early family environments had left their mark in respect of their initial levels of religious observance. A frequent observation made by many parents was their awareness of the relative lack of active and practical involvement of a religious nature in their own families during their childhood years. This lack of active participation may well have been a factor in the decline of religious feeling amongst many parents. This was especially evident when parents commented about their increased observance of Pesach.

From the comments made by the majority of the interviewees there seems little doubt that their own childhood experiences had laid the foundations for either their acceptance or their rejection of later potential influences on their level of religious observance. The examples given appear to reflect varied practices. Yet the data has shown that at the very least these parents were receptive to the early childhood influences that would confront them in later years through their own children.

Examples from the interviews below indicate that there were twelve differing childhood experiences which appear to have been the foundation for increased religious observance in later years, and four which appear to have brought about a lessening of adult religious observance.

Consider this example of experiencing a warm close Jewish family life in childhood, which acted as a positive catalyst in adult life.

'We came from Iraq and what kept us together was really our religion – the tradition. We were never very Orthodox. What kept us together was the tradition. The closeness of our family is very important to us, to both of us, our parents and everybody together.' (101/98)

Another family who had also spent their childhood years in an Arab country found that it was to have a profound effect on their attitude towards Judaism in later years.

'We are very much aware of the point about us being different. Our parents spent all their lives being different. As children we spent our lives being different. With our background we always had to blend in. We seem to blend in with the rest. Maybe as children if we spoke, it would easily distinguish us as being different. So I think, yes, we are very much aware of it.' (125/98)

On the other hand there were several parents who were born in England who had also experienced a warm and positive Jewish environment. The wife of family (108/99) had married a man who came from a relatively non-observant background.

'Both of my parents came from religious families. My mother came from a very religious family, her uncles were Rabbis, and she was very observant. My father was quite observant. In the earlier years we lived in a Jewish community in London. There was no shortage of kosher butchers and kosher delicatessen and my parents were strictly kosher. They had no problems at all. It was just the norm. I went to a Jewish day school and I never knew any different when I was younger. It seemed a very normal life to me. But then religion became square. I was a child, a teenager of the sixties, and I really didn't want to know.' (108/99)

Contrast the above example with the totally strict Orthodox life which caused another parent to reject in later years. The husband, who claimed to be a rebel from an early age, reflected on his life at home:

'I was doing it because of my father. If I was sitting at the table after a meal I would try to say Birkat HaMazon quickly and I would

jump up and my father would kick me. I would go to the synagogue Friday night. I would have a wash and clean my shoes to be able to go to the synagogue on Friday night. Because if I didn't I had an argument with my father. Saturday morning it was the same, but as soon as my father would turn his head, I would go and play football near by the synagogue and come back. So I was doing it I think by fear of not having too much fun with my father when I was young. But as soon as I had the freedom I was not doing it.' (148/99)

He admitted, however, that even though his current level of religious observance was far less than that of his childhood, his early years upbringing had furnished him with a certain degree of strong roots which remained with him.

'I think that it is due to the background. The background was solid with very strong roots and we carried it away with us even from Switzerland to Paris and from Paris to England we have been doing it that way.' (148/99)

He did not completely forsake his past, but felt that he would retain what seemed appropriate and relevant to him, something that his parents would never have condoned.

'To me the Jewish religion is a very large spectrum and I take from it what is suitable for me.' (148/99)

He felt that his own current level of observance was a sincere one. When his father asked him how he could still call himself a Jew if he did not behave like one, his reply was, *'I do it because it's in my heart'.* This is perhaps the main reason why he is willing to encourage his own children to be more religious.

The parent below had also grown up in an Orthodox environment but became attracted to the less religious life of her boyfriend, whom she was later to marry.

'My husband's parents were much less observant than my parents and on Rosh Hashanah I would come over to him sometimes on a Saturday and it upset my parents terribly. I think that remained till I got into my late teens and then I started to feel guilty about it and once I left school and I became more independent minded again and

I grew out of that phase. I never went back to the terribly religious phase I went through as a young teenager. We got married in an Orthodox shul, but again we didn't keep very much when we first got married. We just kept the major festivals, nothing much more than that.' (113/98)

She did however admit that she was determined that her home would always be kosher.

'I think I was fairly emphatic. I think I just said we are going to have kosher meat and that was the end of it. It wasn't an issue.' (113/98)

The positive environmental influence of living in a small but cohesive Jewish community and attendance at a Jewish youth club was also a powerful factor for greater observance in later years.

'We were never Shomer Shabbat, we didn't go to shul regularly. We kept kosher at home, but we ate out. That was about it really. But really my involvement with the Jewish community was the fact that going to a Jewish school my friends tended to be Jewish. Also there was a Jewish youth club which I used to go to very regularly whether it was sporting events or just socially. I got very involved in the Jewish football team. There was a big social scene, again sort of teenager, during my teenage life. And really it was all through the youth club and the Jewish community, which we used to go to. Being a small community, I guess in a sense it was much easier. You knew all the Jewish families there. My parents were not very religious but all their friends tended to be Jewish people. I think that we felt a part of the community, because it wasn't this huge mass of people. It was very small. Everyone really felt a part of the community. So I'd say that I was quite actively involved in the community, although as I said, we were never particularly religious. We got very involved in the community. Our family was very well known within the community. My father was on various committees, Jewish committees which I obviously I got involved with sometimes to a greater or lesser extent.' (132/99)

However, simply living in a Jewish area was itself insufficient if, as the interview below shows, one has experienced growing up in a secular-minded Jewish family.

'Religion didn't have much to do with anything. We all went to state schools, public schools. But again, 99% of the kids there were Jewish. We were brought up in the schools to learn about Chanukah as well as Christmas, Pesach as well as Easter. At home there was everything in the house. Whatever you are not supposed to eat, we ate. But we observed the traditional holidays, Rosh Hashanah and Pesach, the main holidays. On Yom Kippur we all fasted. I have to be honest, the other holidays we never even heard of. We went to synagogue on those holidays but that also petered out when we were still quite young.' (105/98)

With some parents, an early childhood experience of being part of a minority group at school appeared to reinforce their later decision not to allow their own children to have the same problems. Consider the childhood experiences of a woman who was the only Jewish pupil and suffered a degree of discomfort although every effort was made by the school to ensure that this would not occur.

'I didn't go to the Jewish school, and I was the only Jewish girl in a non-Jewish school which was horrible, absolutely awful. It was what they call inter-denominational. It was really sort of 90% Catholic, 9% Protestant and 1% Jewish. So obviously quite a lot of the things they would always do in morning assembly where I'd have to stand there. They knew that I wouldn't participate. You know, it's something that you always remember. I mean I knew every hymn, I just wasn't allowed to sing them. So if it was Pesach or Rosh Hashanah I used to be asked to go to all the classes and give a little talk on it, which was awful because I felt very singled out. You know I'd have to bring the matzah in every year and everybody would taste it and everybody would go "ugh" and I'd stand at the front of the class, it was horrible.' (149/99)

This can be contrasted with another parent who related the following from her childhood experience of being not the sole Jewish pupil but in a minority 'group' at her school.

'On the other hand I went to non-Jewish schools and Jewish people always sought out Jewish people anyway, so we kept our identity in that respect.' (102/99)

In the introduction to this book, I drew attention to research studies in the USA which showed that regardless of being educated at a Jewish day school, Jewish religious identity in adult years was dependent on growing up in a family which supported the values and ethos of the school. This was certainly true of the following parent.

'My Jewish education was twelve years at Jewish day schools. I think that it probably didn't leave me being as religious as it might have, as it should have after twelve years of education, but I suppose my home environment was relatively secular and not that religious, and that played a greater part when I left school in not being that committed to religion.' (103/99)

His admission, however, that his interest in secular Zionism and modern Israel was a catalyst towards being receptive to a more religiously observant life shows a typical example of the close affinity that exists in this case between a political, cultural and religious ideology.

'Maybe I'm understating the value of what the Jewish school gave me because I was imbued with a sense of Zionism for example which I didn't associate directly with Judaism. Yes, I think that's probably the key which has helped me to assert more my Jewish identity.' (103/99)

The tragedy of losing members of the family in the Nazi Holocaust, experiencing the sorrow of bereavement and the search for comfort and meaning at such a traumatic time is often one of the known 'entry points' which can lead into a more religious and personally meaningful lifestyle. Conversely, the tragedy of the Holocaust can cause either rejection or, in some cases, a strengthening of faith of the survivors. Discovering as a teenager that her parents were survivors of the Nazi atrocities had given this parent the stimulus to pass on to her own children the need to develop a strong Jewish identity.

'It has had a very profound effect on my life. I wanted to make sure that all my children knew about it. Perhaps, in more detail than another parent would have passed it on, but I felt that it was very important at a very early age.' (128/99)

In other families, an early sense of Jewish identity was established through the experience of family bereavement. Consider the following comment from a parent.

'Within the family I was always the one that tended to be more religious than the rest. I'm not quite sure what the real motivation was, why I am built that way, more suggestible, I don't know. The ritual and the drama, I really don't know what the primitive motivations were. But I think I started to get more religious when my mother was dying. My initial reaction on the day she died was we've got to do the right thing. What's the right thing? I was very much more focused, not on the medics, what I could or couldn't do for my mother at that point, but rather to the Rabbi. What was the right thing to do? I was certain that it had to be followed.' (135/99)

In the interviews, there were many examples of parents who had themselves experienced a traditional Jewish family life and wished to recreate this with their own children. However, the parents who grew up amongst a more secular non-observant family had no such 'religious' nostalgia which they wished to emulate. This was especially true in the case of those whose wider family and friends were themselves non-observant.

With this group of families, evidence from the data points to other reasons which brought about a decision to send their children to a Jewish day school. These reasons were frequently socially based and were invariably due to the influence of friends or the community where it was the norm amongst many families to send the children to a Jewish school.

'My parents kept almost nothing at all. I would go to shul on Rosh Hashanah and Yom Kippur. We'd go inside a shul if there was a Bar Mitzvah or a wedding in the family or of close friends. But that was about it. I was sent to cheder. I think that my parents belonged to an Orthodox shul when I was very young and then they joined the Reform. As I said they kept very little. My father, my mother has passed away, keeps nothing really to this day. Once I was a teenager, nearly all my friends, well virtually all my friends, were Jewish and nearly all of them were members of families that belonged to the Orthodox shul. So it was through my friends, and going to their homes that I got any exposure at all to Jewish culture.' (108/99)

The above parent was introduced to a more religious Jewish life when he married a woman who came from a more observant family. He continued as follows:

34

'We knew each other for seven years before we got married. So it was inevitable I suppose that I would be drawn more into religious life. My father-in-law was, he was observant, but he was tolerant. I would actually enjoy going with him. We would go together on the High Holidays. Before we had children we would spend Rosh Hashanah at my in-laws. I would go to shul with my father-in-law. That was the first time I was introduced to a shul and I felt welcomed. That was it. He introduced me to everybody, so immediately I was welcomed in as one of the community. That made a huge difference and by the time we got married I felt really at home there and knew everybody and of course going to shul more than I'd ever done in my life. I was actually beginning to pick things up. I was never much good at reading, I'm not good now, but I was a lot better by the time we got married than I had been in my earlier life, even when I was at cheder. So that was how I got drawn more into a religious sphere.' (108/99)

The influence of non-religious friends in one's youth was certainly the cause of a negative influence on their own level of religious observance as in the following statement from one parent who felt that the influence of his friends and acquaintances had encouraged him to lessen his level of religious observance:

'I went out from it very slowly because of the people I was mixing with and so on.' (127/99)

In another family, the wife commented that when she was a child, her parents attended the synagogue on the Sabbath and kept a kosher home but they also moved further away from the Jewish community. As most of her school friends were not Jewish, she did not generally mix socially with the local Jewish community.

'Then I went to secretarial college and that was when all sort of the troubles really started between me and mum and dad. Because obviously I've been brought up with this sort of mixing out rather than in and of course their big night out was Friday night. So I'd want to go out on a Friday night, but Friday night was Shabbat so it always led to an argument, always if I wanted to go out and I wasn't allowed to. Some Friday nights I did.' (126/99)

A common theme throughout all the interviews was the awareness of many parents of the contrast between the relative lack of active and practical involvement of a religious nature in their own families during their childhood years and their current more religious life style. It seems clear from the above varied examples of the childhood experiences of the majority of these parents that regardless of their initial level of adult religious observance, they were, at the very least, receptive to the later influences that would confront them through their own children. With this in mind, it is important to establish and understand the various reasons which prompted so many parents to send their children to a Jewish day school.

Chapter 4

Why parents chose a Jewish primary school for their children

The decision to send their child to a Jewish day school may well be a starting point for many less religious families on the road to greater religious observance. Indeed, it can be said that those who decide to send their children to such a school have already taken this step. But what are the 'main reasons' why parents chose to send their children to a Jewish day school? It is perhaps understandable that the more religious families would make such a choice, but what of the less or non-religious families? What reasons might they have for making such a choice?

Primarily and logically, one might assume that most parents are likely to focus on the desire for their children to experience the combination of a good secular and Jewish education in a happy, strong and positive Jewish environment. Regardless, however, of their initial reasons for selecting a Jewish day school, it is by no means certain or expected that the religious life style of the parents will change. Nor indeed might the parents themselves anticipate that it would have any practical effect on their own lives. A closer inspection of the reasons given by those less or non-religious families who selected a Jewish primary school will provide useful information.

Questionnaire responses

The questionnaire suggested six possible reasons why parents would choose a Jewish primary school for their children. The responses are listed below in order of parental priority. The percentage figures give the average of all three schools combined.

81% – wanted their children to read Hebrew and follow a synagogue service.

69% – wanted their children to have Jewish friends.

61% – wanted their children to learn to speak Ivrit (Modern Hebrew).

55% – were already observant and the school reflected their way of life.

55% – wanted to give their children the type of education that they had received.

54% – wanted to give their children the type of education that they had not received.

There may be two reasons for the high number (81%) who were anxious for their children to read Hebrew and to follow a synagogue service. Firstly, it may be prompted by the feeling of inadequacy of those parents who have difficulty with Hebrew reading and following a synagogue service themselves. Secondly, there are parents whose knowledge and ability are far higher and who expect their children to reach the same standard. It is interesting to note that this percentage of parents who rated this as 'important' was higher than those who wanted their children to be able to learn and to speak Modern Hebrew (61%).

Approximately the same percentage of parents chose a Jewish primary school for their children either because one or both parents had received a Jewish primary school education and wanted their children to experience the same, or because they wanted their children to benefit from an education that they themselves had not received. Both areas show a positive attitude towards Jewish primary schools which is explored in greater depth during the interviews.

One possible reason which had been omitted from the questionnaire became a major reason given by the majority of parents during the interviews: the wish for their children to obtain a sound Jewish identity. This will be developed in greater detail below.

Parents were also asked to comment on three possible reasons why they did not select a non-Jewish or multicultural school. The percentage figures give the average of all three schools combined.

50% – did not wish their child to participate in other religious practices.

18% – were concerned about discrimination at non-Jewish schools.

12% – did not wish their child to learn about other religions.

These questionnaire responses indicate that although many parents did not wish their children to participate in the religious practices of other faiths, an even larger percentage of parents felt this to be unimportant. Evidence from the interviews below suggests that many parents whose children attend Jewish day schools would in fact welcome the idea of their children learning more about other religions and being more aware of living in a multicultural society.

Interview responses

Eight main reasons for choosing a Jewish primary school were given by parents during interviews:

1. Importance of obtaining a sound Jewish identity.
2. Parent felt he/she had missed out on a Jewish education.
3. Parent(s) had attended and benefited from a Jewish day school.
4. Religious and secular studies are both a natural part of the curriculum.
5. The children of friends of parents attended and recommended the school.
6. It was important for a social and community foundation.
7. It was seen to have a warm and special Jewish family atmosphere.
8. A parental substitute for those who could not offer the Jewish dimension at home.

Reason 1: Importance of obtaining a sound Jewish identity

Almost all the families who were interviewed stated that they had chosen a Jewish day school, trusting that it would provide not only a sound Jewish education but, even more important, the foundations for a positive 'Jewish identity'. These families appeared to view the influence of the school, and not necessarily their own parental influence, as the main basis for their children developing a strong sense of Jewish identity.

Several felt that, ultimately, the decision of how the children would lead their adult lives would have to be left to the individual children. A Jewish school, however, would at least give them the basic foundation on which to make an informed choice.

There was also a feeling by many parents that a Jewish day school was a form of 'buying insurance' to avoid the chances of intermarriage in later years.

- *'We thought that by sending them to a Jewish school the chances were that they would grow up with a good knowledge of how Jewish people should live.' (107/99)*

- *'I wanted him to know who he was and what club he belonged to and to identify with that.' (133/99)*

- *'A Jewish school would be able to teach them the things that we could not.' (134/99)*

- *'A Jewish school would be able to provide a Jewish ethos in their life every day.' (128/99)*

- *'Knowing about the moral values is what makes a decent human being, that's the most important. That's what we really wanted from a Jewish school: that they taught them how to behave in a world that doesn't any more.' (109/98)*

- *'We needed to stress Jewish education; otherwise the children could easily grow up and not carry on their Jewish tradition. You have got to give them the values for them to then make their own decision in life.' (134/99)*

- *'If they are to have any chance not to marry out it would be more chance for them if they went to a Jewish school.' (136/99)*

- *'I didn't want him to come home with Easter bunnies and Christmas cards. I thought that at the age of five he wouldn't understand why we didn't have Christmas. I felt that at five, children are too impressionable and say: "Why don't we have Christmas? Why can't I go to Jonnie's party at the local beefburger restaurant?" Whereas if he then went to a non-Jewish secondary school, by the age of eleven he would understand the reasons.' (110/99)*

- *'We decided that to get the Jewish primary education was important. Then, maybe later on when it came to choosing secondary school, that might be a different matter. Maybe then we wouldn't choose a Jewish school.' (118/98)*

Reason 2: Parent felt he/she had missed out on a Jewish education

Many parents felt that they wanted to give their children the opportunity to benefit from a Jewish day school education that they themselves had not received. There was a feeling of having 'missed out' on their Jewish education. This feeling of having 'missed out' was a major factor with all of the families who, when younger, had attended the part-time 'cheder' system but felt that they had not benefited from it.

- *'I grew up in a very non-Jewish environment and I wanted to give them the experience of going to a Jewish school which I hadn't received myself. But at the end of the day I've never looked at any other schools. I think that it was because I wanted the children to have a Jewish education because I didn't have one.' (111/99)*

- *'I never went to a Jewish school and I thought I missed out. Although my grandparents were ultra-Orthodox, my parents weren't. I wanted to give my kids a start that I felt I didn't have. I went through the cheder system and I hardly learned anything.' (114/98)*

- *'Cheder was a waste of time for me and if that's what we are going to do for Emma, sending her to a secular school and trying to send her to cheder and all the rest of it, it just wouldn't work.' (138/99)*

- *'From my point of view I had no Jewish education at all when I was younger, no cheder, nothing, so I felt I missed out. So I wanted her to have what I really didn't have.' (128/98)*

- *'I was always aware that I was in a tiny minority and I didn't really want my children to have to go through that.' (130/99)*

Reason 3: Parent(s) had attended and benefited from a Jewish day school

The following comments from interviews emphasise the feelings of happiness and benefit received by parents and their desire to ensure that their children experience the same.

- *'I really enjoyed my years there, a very happy time.' (115/99)*

- *'I ended up very knowledgeable and I thought that was a very valuable experience.' (119/98)*

- *'I thought that I would like my children to have the same sort of happy experience that I had.' (129/98)*

- *'It's not just about feeling safe, it's about feeling secure and it's about being happy.' (120/99)*

Many of the families from Brook primary school had an additional reason for sending their children. This school, unlike Rubin and Norton, can be termed a community school. It is situated in the heart of the area where most of the Jewish families live, and most families, whether observant or not, felt that sending their children to Brook was *'a foregone conclusion.'*

- *'It is such a small community that everybody knows everyone else.' (139/99)*

- *'The children that my own kids mix with, they've known most of them since they were tiny, and because they are all going there, you tend to group together and all go to the same place.' (144/99)*

- *'The people that you socialise with, that you grew up with and that got married at the same time as you and had children at the same time as you, they are all going to send their children to that school.' (146/99)*

Reason 4: Religious and secular studies are both a natural part of the curriculum

Many of the families interviewed felt that one of the main attractions of a Jewish day school was the natural fusion of Jewish education into the school curriculum, especially if the school is a part of the state system where the full National Curriculum would be taught.

- *'When you operate in a non-Jewish world it was very important to me that they had been to a state school yet it was also a Jewish school. So you could actually combine being normal and not being marginal and being Jewish.' (116/99)*

- *'A Jewish school is the best of both worlds. In a sense it was an easy decision to make because they were getting two for the price of one as it were.' (122/99)*

- *'The secular standards have to be the same or as good as all the other schools.' (131/99)*

- *'Things are incorporated naturally into the school curriculum without having to go to cheder and take time out.' (125/98)*

All the parents stated that if they had sent their children to a non-Jewish school they would still want them to receive some form of a Jewish education. At a Jewish day school there was the added advantage of not having to send the children to a part-time cheder on Sundays or after school hours on weekdays.

Another important reason was given by more observant parents who would have to ask for special privileges if their children were at a non-Jewish school.

- *'We didn't want to send them to a school where they would have to make excuses to have early Fridays.' (117/98)*

- *'There would always be a kosher meal for them and we wouldn't have that to worry about.' (123/99)*

- *'It's all the things that we would keep in the house. If they went to a non-Jewish school you've got to start thinking about lots of things. It's just a lot less hassle.' (119/98)*

Reason 5: The recommendation of friends

Data from interviews with parents of children at Brook primary school confirmed that they had been influenced by their friends who had chosen that school for their own children. It was, as stated above, seen to be the local Jewish community school.

- *'I think that with all our circle of friends we all sent our children to Brook primary school, so there was no other choice really.' (136/99)*

- *'The children of all our friends go there. The children of old friends that my husband and I went to school with. They all go to the same school as we did.' (124/99)*

- *'There wasn't any choice. It was never discussed. That was where my children were going from the very beginning. I suppose it's where all their friends have gone.' (140/99)*

- *'We were also persuaded by the actions of our friends who had older children and were supporting the structure.' (145/99)*

Reason 6: Important for a social and community foundation

The comments made in the interviews below were echoed by many others.

- *'I see a Jewish school in the same way that I see any Jewish person within the community as having a wider role within that community in the sense of being a focal point for all parents. A focal point for kids to mix with their own kind and parents to mix with their own kind. Because at the end of the day if you don't mix with your own kind you are not going to be able to guarantee survival I suppose.' (146/99)*

- *'We have a whole circle of friends now through the children.' (104/98)*

- *'There is a bonding between Jewish people.' (126/99)*

- *'The people you mix with have been brought up in the same way as you.' (142/99)*

- *'They've got their Jewishness in common, they can see each other socially. The culture being the same.' (133/99)*

The above comments were closely linked with the increased opportunity and encouragement for them and their families to remain within the fold. The essential core factor here is the idea of the school being not merely a place of education for the children but also a 'focal point' for Jewish parents as well as children to meet and mix socially within their own religious group. Parents felt that it was important for them to develop social contact with other similar families. This is not an unusual occurrence and is quite common at all primary schools throughout the country. The important factor to note here, however, is that all the friendships made are between Jewish families.

Reason 7: A warm and special atmosphere

I have no doubt that the great majority of all primary schools throughout the country are warm and happy environments for the children. Nevertheless, parents commented on what they considered was a *'very special atmosphere at a Jewish primary school'*.

- *'It's like a village school in a way where everybody knows each other and all the teachers know you. It's almost like Auntie Whoever rather than Mrs Whoever.' (141/99)*

- *'It's just a nice warm feeling when we go there. There's a very special atmosphere at a Jewish primary school. I noticed it when I was a child. My husband didn't notice it until he started going to the school functions. He said that there was a very special warm atmosphere.' (122/99)*

- *'You're all in it together. All the parents and all the children and most of the teachers all have a common link, a common bond that is very strong.' (126/99)*

- *'I just felt that it was like a community-type school. I like it. I feel very much at home and comfortable there.' (143/99)*

It is quite likely that many of the parents interviewed would have felt the same about any other primary school that their children attended.

Yet it appears from the comments made by parents of pupils attending a Jewish primary school that this factor was especially noticeable. It may well have to do with the attraction and comfort of knowing that all the parents, regardless of their level of observance, all had the same religion and culture.

It is interesting to note the comments of the family below who had moved their child from a multicultural state primary school to a Jewish primary school. According to the parents, the young child, without knowing it was a Jewish primary school, felt the difference.

'We never said to her we are taking you out of your school and we are sending you to a Jewish school. We just said to her, right, you are going to go here because it's closer. Anyway on the Monday she went to school and when she came out I said, "Well what do you think?" I never ever mentioned about it being a Jewish school. She said to me, the people are so so different. She was five years old. She said that they are so different and I feel so much happier. And it's amazing how a child can pick up on that. And we have never looked back, never.' (112/98)

Reason 8: A parental substitute

The final reason for choosing a Jewish primary school that was given by parents during interviews related to the self-awareness of some parents that, in connection with Jewish education, the school was a substitute for the parents. For some parents the school was able to offer what they could not offer, because of a lack of adequate knowledge.

'Neither my wife nor myself were particularly observant and what we were able to teach the children was always going to be less than what a Jewish school would be able to provide. There were numerous reasons. I knew that I would never have the time to give them the Jewish education, because I was travelling all the time. My wife couldn't because she didn't have the knowledge. So I passed that responsibility to the school. You could call it benefit from two sides: first is the lazy one, that we wouldn't have to do the teaching. Secondly we would learn from them which has been the case.' (128/98)

Another parent who could perhaps have imparted a sound Jewish education at home was still happy to leave it to the school.

> *'I see the school as almost being like a parental substitute in the sense that they do so much for the children in Jewish education. It leaves us with very little that we have to do to teach them. They get it from the school. It's a part of their daily life.' (121/99)*

Conclusions from the above data relating to the reasons given by parents for the choice of a Jewish day school

The decision made by parents to send their children to a Jewish day school was clearly connected with a number of other related issues which reflected the parents' philosophy and attitude to Judaism. All the parents expressed a personal love and pride for Judaism and the hope that their children would develop the same feeling.

To sum up, I found that there were four main reasons given by parents for choosing a Jewish primary school for their children:

1. The importance of maintaining a Jewish identity. This had a twofold purpose. Firstly, in a positive sense, to develop a love and pride of being Jewish, and secondly, to act as a buffer against intermarriage.

2. To provide a sound Jewish education, either as a substitute for the parents' inadequate Jewish knowledge or to reflect the earlier Jewish education of the parents.

3. To provide the benefit of a combination of secular and Jewish religious education within the normal school day with no additional burden of arranging for Jewish education out of the normal school hours.

4. To provide the Jewish family atmosphere of a warm and happy environment. There was also a sense of comfort for parents knowing that all the families, regardless of their level of observance, had the same religion and culture. To this was added the communal benefits with the school acting as a catalyst and focal point for increased parental and family contact with other Jewish families in the community.

Chapter 5

In which ways did the parents increase their religious observance?

As pointed out in Chapter 1, none of the parents had expected that their own levels of religious observance would increase because their children would be attending a Jewish day school. This chapter focuses on the responses to the questionnaires and interviews and shows the areas where parents' religious observance had increased. In the following chapter I will examine the specific reasons for these increases.

Questionnaires

The questionnaire focused on eleven specific areas of religious observance which were selected for two main reasons. Firstly, they are representative of the most commonly practised areas of Jewish religious observance. Secondly, it may be possible to show relevant links with similar learning activities of the children at their schools.

The eleven areas are:

1. Observance of dietary laws at home.
2. Observance of dietary laws away from home.
3. Lighting Shabbat candles on Friday night.
4. Shabbat Kiddush recited at home.
5. Synagogue attendance on Shabbat.
6. Havdalah ceremony observed at home.
7. During Pesach: eating only kosher for Pesach food.

8. Participating in a full Pesach seder.
9. Attending synagogue on Pesach, Shavuot and Sukkot.
10. Lighting a menorah at Chanukah.
11. Having a sukkah at home on Sukkot.

For the sake of clarity, I have listed below only the final percentage of the increases in religious observance of parents in each school in each of the above eleven areas. **It will be seen that there has been a noticeable increase in the level of observance in every area.**

Two main questions formed the basis of this data:

Q4. What is the level of your religious observance today in each of the areas listed?

Q5. When you were adult but before you were married, what was your level of religious observance in each of the areas listed?

Where applicable, the figures below refer either to the percentage increase in the level of religious observance of the whole family or to that of husbands and wives separately.

The increase in the observance of dietary laws at home

Rubin: 22.6%   Norton: 32.7%   Brook: 14.0%

The increase in the observance of dietary laws away from home.

Husbands: Rubin 22.1%   Norton 26.9%   Brook 22.1%
Wives: Rubin 22.9%   Norton 26.9%   Brook 17.5%

In the observance of the dietary laws outside of the home, there is a similar **average overall increase** of 22.6% for men and 21.4% for women. This is particularly interesting and relevant in respect of men. One would perhaps have expected a lower level of religious observance from the majority of men, since it is suggested that they are likely to be more lax in this respect due to the pressure of business and work commitments. The same could of course apply to working women, although it is likely that the majority of women who responded to the questionnaire had young children and were less likely to have the same degree of external work commitments as their husbands.

There appear to be many factors which contribute to this increase in the observance of the dietary laws and all are examined in greater depth in the interviews. The figures above, however, indicate quite clearly that an increase of observance has taken place and later information through the interviews will highlight the role that the children and the school have played in this respect.

The increase in lighting Shabbat candles on Friday night

Rubin: 17.2%   Norton: 21.3%   Brook: 10.0%

The relatively lower figures, when compared to other areas of increased observance, may well be caused by the in-built tradition and custom of lighting Shabbat candles found even amongst less religious families.

The increase in the Shabbat Kiddush recited at home on Friday nights

Rubin: 25.1%   Norton: 24.9%   Brook: 25.6%

The increase in synagogue attendance on Shabbat

Husbands:	Rubin 23.8%	Norton 23.0%	Brook 15.1%
Wives:	Rubin 9.1%	Norton 27.0%	Brook 9.2%

The increase of the Havdalah ceremony observed at home.

Rubin: 14.3%   Norton: 19.2%   Brook: 8.7%

The increase in eating only kosher for Pesach food during Pesach

Husbands:	Rubin 17.2%	Norton 19.3%	Brook 4.7%
Wives:	Rubin 18.8%	Norton 19.3%	Brook 15.1%

The increase in participating in a full Pesach seder

Rubin: 7.8%   Norton: 13.5%   Brook: 15.1%

There are some interesting comparisons to be made here. There appears to be little change in the level of observance of families who participate in a full seder service. The reason for this may be due to the high percentage of families who claimed to have attended a full seder in previous years:

Rubin: 89.7%   Norton: 86.5%   Brook: 79.0%

Pesach has now become a traditional occasion for families to get together on an annual basis regardless of the level of observance of each member of the family. Many families are likely to have used the traditional seder service printed in the Haggadah as the basis for the evening's celebrations, although the depth of religious content of each seder service is likely to differ. This may well be the reason why so many families stated that they had always attended a 'full seder service'.

The increase in synagogue attendance on Pesach, Shavuot and Sukkot

Husbands: Rubin 30.4%   Norton 23.1%   Brook 11.6%
Wives: Rubin 26.3%   Norton 26.9%   Brook 18.6%

The increase of observance in this category is of particular significance since on many occasions it necessitates not going to work on weekdays. Observance of the New Year (Rosh Hashanah) and the Day of Atonement (Yom Kippur) was not included in the survey since, traditionally, the great majority of families will be likely to attend the synagogue on these occasions. It is an established and well-known fact that, in what are termed 'Central Orthodox synagogues', attendance on the Three Pilgrim or Foot Festivals of Pesach, Shavuot and Sukkot is without doubt considerably less than on Rosh Hashanah and Yom Kippur and any increase of observance on these days would certainly imply a greater religious commitment. Only the more observant will not go to work on Pesach, Shavuot and Sukkot. The increase in synagogue attendance on these days, and which is confirmed by the interviews below, is a clear indication that more families are taking time off work in order to take their children to the synagogue on those occasions.

The increase of families lighting a menorah at Chanukah

Rubin: 23.8%   Norton: 19.2%   Brook: 23.9%

There is once again a significant increase of observance from parents in all three schools. Additional data from the interviews will show that the increase of observance of lighting a menorah at Chanukah is due mainly to the wish to involve the children in this ritual which they learn about at school and talk about at home. Many families during interviews admitted that if it were not for the children they would not have observed these occasions with the same zeal. Nevertheless, it is interesting to note the relatively large percentage of families who had always lit a menorah at Chanukah even if they did not consider themselves to be 'observant'. I feel that this has much to do with the wish of many parents to retain a sense of 'Jewish identity' in their lives. This ritual is relatively easy to observe as it requires no other commitment other than possessing a menorah and lighting it at home when it gets dark.

The increase in families having a sukkah at home on Sukkot

Rubin: 18.1%   Norton:30.7%   Brook: 19.1%

The increase in observance here is of particular significance as it implies a strong commitment related to the need for considerable physical and, in some cases, financial involvement. The building of a sukkah at home can be a strenuous DIY effort or can be made relatively easy with the purchase of an easily erectable ready-made sukkah. There is still a need for careful planning and preparation to enable it to be decorated, furnished and ready for use for meals. As with other Jewish rituals, many families during interviews admitted that if it were not for the children they would not have even considered the possibility of building a sukkah at home.

The questionnaire responses have indicated a clear and positive increase in the level of religious observance in every one of the areas examined. Each category is examined again in far greater detail during the course of the in-depth interviews with parents.

Interviews

Sometimes it is better to let the data do the talking. The excerpts below are examples of the actual responses of the families who were interviewed. These families had already indicated on the completed questionnaires that their level of religious observance had increased during the time that their children had been pupils at a Jewish primary school. They now had the opportunity to talk about the specific areas where changes had taken place.

Synagogue attendance

'I think that, probably, the greatest area that's had an effect has been me going to shul on certain holidays where I or we might not have gone. It's partly the fact that they are off school then. That's prompted us again when they say that there has been some build up at school.' (132/99)

'From our point of view it was the children that taught me how to follow the reading of the Torah which I never knew before. Who was called up? I never understood any of it. My children have taught me and I understood it quickly, being older. Having learned from the older one I can now ask the little one, why are we doing this and so on.' (129/98)

'I wanted to be able to follow more things that they followed. I wanted to be able to sit in the synagogue and say to the children: this is where we are, this is the place. I wanted to be able to follow it and not to be completely lost. I want to be able to show them something. So when our daughter was about six or seven I felt that I wanted to improve my understanding of Hebrew reading, so I went on a Hebrew reading course. I'd never have thought of doing that before. (114/98)

'We became more involved with the shul. We knew that at school they were learning about Shabbat and going to shul and I felt that it would be sensible if I took them there for the children's service. But

after a while I got used to going and I enjoyed being there myself.' *(105/98)*

'Now, I go because I want to and enjoy it, but to begin with it was certainly because of the children. I wanted them to experience the Shabbat at shul that they were learning about in school. When we moved, we wanted to live near the synagogue for the sake of the children and ourselves.' (101/98)

'Before the children were at school, we would never have gone. My husband and I would have gone for Rosh Hashanah, Yom Kippur and that's all. I suppose I would go for myself as well. I feel like, well if they are not going into school, they're not going to sit in front of the television, and for me as well. I also feel the last six months or whatever, whenever we've gone to the shul, whereas before I'd be quite happy to go into the children's service, have the Kiddush and then go home. Now I will go into the main shul, say my prayers and feel that I am saying what I want to say while they go to the children's services on their own. It would be a lot easier for me just to go into the children's service because I wouldn't have to do anything. But I feel that I want to go into shul. And I think that's for myself.' (134/99)

But it was not quite the same for her husband.

'I don't know if I go to shul any more than I used to. I probably still go on High Holidays. No more than that. Although I will probably start taking the kids on a Shabbat a bit more because I think they want to go. Although, having said that, I'd feel happy that I'd taken my children. I would feel very comfortable in the fact that I've taken my children and that to me would be a sense of achievement. That I've actually taken my children and I've gone on a Shabbat.' (134/99)

I can speak with first-hand experience of seeing dozens of families with young children attending my own synagogue every Shabbat. With very few exceptions, all the children are pupils at Jewish day schools. I have no doubt that a similar situation is found at almost every synagogue where children have the opportunity to attend a Jewish primary school.

Synagogue members with good memories will be able to confirm that this was not always the case. It is no coincidence that the proliferation of Jewish primary schools has gone hand in hand with increased synagogue attendance of the families.

Sabbath observance

'They have encouraged us to sing Zemirot at the Shabbat table and to bench at the end of the meal. They love teaching us all the songs they learn at school. We have stopped watching the TV on Shabbat and have made a proper Shabbat atmosphere for them because it seems that it is the way they enjoy and now so do we. Due to the children we don't cook or drive on Shabbat. We have a time switch for the lights. We try to do most things but we are not extreme ultra religious.' (102/99)

'We did observe Shabbat before they were born, but now we feel that we are doing it for a purpose. When there were just two of us, we wondered why we are doing it. When the children are involved it seems much more important. Everything we do is because of them, or we wouldn't have done it. They have taught us. With the children's service and the things from school. They've taught us and I now think that we've picked it up for ourselves.' (106/98)

'Certainly now Shabbat is Shabbat on a Friday night. I light the candles, the children light candles, we make Kiddush, we have a nice dinner. But when there was just the two of us, I don't think there was any difference to any other night of the week. The Friday night has now become a part of us.' (130/99)

'There must be a knock-on effect of the children becoming more observant and saying, we don't want to do this on Shabbat, and we shouldn't be doing this. So there is that kind of indirect effect.' (135/99)

'From the time that our daughter first started at school, since she started, we started using a Shabbat urn and we had a time switch fitted. Also we stopped using the phone on Shabbat. I have actually found it harder than I thought I would. It was a very drastic change for me. We made a decision and we just did it. But it was the children who were saying that you shouldn't press buttons on Shabbat. These were drastic changes.' (124/99)

'I didn't always get home on a Friday on time before Shabbat and now, it's only for the last four or five years that I do so. It was very difficult to get home early in time for Shabbat particularly in the winter. But because of the children I made a decision. That's it, from now on I am going home early on Friday.' (107/99)

The above comments are certainly indicative of increased Sabbath observance, but once again it is apparent that a high degree of compromise is involved within the majority of families whose level of Sabbath observance has increased. Only a minority of the families who participated in the research can be said to be fully observant in every aspect. Few were prepared to make the ***'drastic changes'*** made by one of the above families. The majority of families were however prepared and willing to change their life-style. In every case a similar reason was given – it was because of the children: ***'Everything we do is because of them, or we wouldn't have done it.'***

Passover observance

One of the highlights of the spring term in many Jewish primary schools is without doubt the 'Demonstration Seder' with all the children participating. This is usually the culmination of several weeks of learning and preparation in the classroom. I remember the first day of the summer term when I was still in my first year of teaching Jewish Studies at a Jewish primary school. When I arrived at the school a parent was waiting for me. Thirty years later I can still remember every word she said:

'I want to thank you for helping us to have the best seder we have ever had in our family. Every year up to now we have gone to our parents and listened to a straight reading of the Haggadah, sang

some songs and ate the food. It was usually boring. But this year it was different because our young daughter seemed to take over. She taught us wonderful songs and told us some great stories about Pesach. It was really lovely. Thank you – thank you.'

She left me with tears in her eyes. Since that day I have received many similar comments year after year. I have no doubt that teachers at other Jewish primary schools have similar experiences. I was therefore not at all surprised to hear the following comments when I interviewed parents as a part of this research study.

'Thanks to what the children have learned at school, we have a really lovely seder. We do some parts in Hebrew and some in English but always we stop to explain and of course to listen to our children who have always something to tell us about a part of the seder or to teach us a new song. It is all so lovely and so different and all thanks to the school. It has really changed our lives.' (115/99)

'When we first got married we bought a box of matzah and that was it. Now, because of the children, it's everything. Subconsciously we both probably felt that we should do a bit more.' (109/98)

'I've never done a Pesach at home as we've always been away. But we did one Pesach and the kids were insistent. They wanted the closets cleaned out. They wanted the chametz out of the house. They wanted new dishes and knives and forks. To me, I was easy. If the bread was out of the house, fine. Dishes are dishes. They wouldn't eat off that. Actually that's the one holiday they wanted. Are we cleaning the rooms thoroughly? Did you sell the chametz? I've never sold chametz in my life. That was the one time in my life where I actually remember all of them they were making a stand there. So we didn't use the dishes. We used paper and plastic. Why do things to upset them if it can be done and it's feasible and it makes them happy? Absolutely, I don't think that we've said no to anything they wanted like that. I would always let them do it.' (140/99)

'On Pesach they were correcting us on various things. They knew about the service, they knew about the plagues and they were able

to do quite a few of the songs and obviously Ma Nishtana they had a fight over who was going to do Ma Nishtana because they all wanted to do it.' (137/99)

'It is lovely on Pesach at the seder. They always seem to take over, with the songs and stories they have learned, it is really lovely.' (131/99)

'We do a proper seder night now. Because they know the songs so well, it seems a shame not to give them the opportunity to repeat it. Also they like to help to make everything, so although it's terrific mad hard work for me we've tightened up on the seders. My husband never had proper seders. His father was very ill and often in bed upstairs and he was the boy downstairs and used to have a telly under the table and make a mockery of it. He never knew how to participate fully. But now we take it very seriously because the kids take it very seriously in school. They all know the songs very well and are particular about singing all the songs. So we do it properly, as properly as we are able.' (123/99)

'What I love about it is when we get the song sheet from school and then we've got something to sing because I've forgotten. They have started to do a little bit more. We are not just singing or saying the blessings like we were doing at school, they are actually singing the folk songs and more in tune with what the kids are singing in Israel. Because we lived there and I know what the kids do over there.' (110/99)

'Our seder night is all about which songs to sing, which tune to use, because they've learned a different tune in school to the one that we know. I remember Rachel was very angry that her Grandma wouldn't let her sing the way she had learned at school. And Rachel of course is also very competent and wanted to be able to lead a lot at the seder night services. Our parents find that quite difficult to accept because they still think that it should be the head of the household and they can't quite grasp the concept that in order to involve the children and make it more interesting for them the more they do and it makes it more fun.' (119/98)

'Every year we have our family round. I decided very early on that the seder would be dictated from what they knew from school. So before anything takes place, I sit down with the girls and we go through absolutely everything they know, song wise, what parts they do. We basically just reaffirm everything they do at school at our seder.' (113/98)

'We had Yom Tov with my niece and nephew, my brother's children who don't go to a Jewish school. They haven't got a breeze what it's all about. And in fact last year at Pesach time the children were singing "Dayenu", one of the songs, and my niece turned round to my sister-in-law and said, "what is she saying – what is she talking about?"' (117/98)

'I remember my son a few years ago telling me off because I didn't prepare for Pesach properly. I hadn't scoured this or swept this. I remember one year, I can't tell you which year it was, that I lined all the shelves with paper and I had done all the changing of the crockery and cutlery, and it still wasn't enough. He went through a phase. I remember, he drove me mad that year. He is the one that was most interested at that particular age. He still is. He is very lively in debates at his school. But he had a tremendous influence at Pesach time as that was all very important to him.' (122/99)

'It was my husband's first seder that he was taking two years ago. There were chunks that he didn't know, and the children said things like, "I know that one, I can do that page, I learned that" and so on. When we got to Grace after Meals we all chipped in, and when we came to Hallel, they had done a chunk at school. And after Hallel we got to the tricky bits and we handed it over to them. So they did a huge part. But last year my husband was pretty good leading it on his own. It's very satisfying to get past that stage and to be able to do it all instead of just sitting there. To me, that's entirely down to the children.' (136/99)

'The children have taught us lovely tunes. My father still sings the tunes of sixty years ago and now they've got like these real hippy

tunes. They do benching to the Match of the Day tune, it's more modern and because it's brought up to date they are more interested in it. The way I was taught at cheder, we weren't interested in it. I guess that more so this year than before they both actively wanted to get involved in the service. It was because they'd learned it at school.' (146/99)

The dietary laws

'The children always seem to know what they may eat or not eat. They have learned about these things at school and they want to keep these laws at home. They are very careful especially when other people offer them food and this has also made it important for us to do the same.' (137/99)

'I think that when I'm shopping now, I'm more careful, whereas before I just picked up packets of biscuits, now I look to see what is written on them. I can't cheat any more. At Pesach I have got to do the Pesach plate and they come in and check that everything has got a hechsher on and that all the cooking things and the dishes are changed over.' (139/99)

'I think that it's in the Jewish dietary laws where we have had the most direct conflicts. I think it's a case of my wife's arm being twisted far enough so that she now does with less complaining than she used to buying what our son is happy with. I think that we've now settled into a pattern. One has to make the decision as to whether you're going to be totally kosher everywhere or not or try and do the best you can. And there is always the danger, I'm well aware of when you are doing the best you can, you are not doing enough because you can do more.' (145/99)

It is evident from the above analysis of the data that the great majority of the parents had increased their own level of religious observance in many areas. The following chapter examines the reasons that prompted these changes to occur.

Chapter 6

The reasons for the increase in the parents' level of religious observance

Question 9 of the questionnaire related to parents whose level of observance had increased during the time that their children attended the primary school. They were asked to indicate whether any specific areas of behaviour of their children or aspects of the school had influenced them towards this higher level of observance.

For the majority of parents from all three schools, the three main factors that have had maximum influence on their own religious attitudes and practice are:

- **the children's religious activity at home**

- **the conversation of their children at home**

- **the wish of parents to support the ethos of the school.**

The figures below indicate the actual percentage of families in each school who considered this as a major source of influence on their own level of religious observance.

Children's religious activity at home:

Rubin: 39.3%   Norton: 34.6%   Brook: 37.4%

Children's conversation at home:

Rubin: 36.0%   Norton: 19.2%   Brook: 30.4%

The wish to support the ethos of the school:

Rubin: 36.0%   Norton: 23.1%   Brook: 27.1%

The three tables below give a comparative percentage order of the areas of maximum influence as indicated on the questionnaire by the parents of each school.

Rubin table of maximum influence

%

39.3 Influence related to children's religious activity at home.
36.0 Influence related to children's conversation at home.
36.0 Influence due to a wish to support the ethos of the school.
26.2 Influence related to attending school assemblies etc.
22.1 Influence related to children learning to speak Ivrit.
21.3 Influence of children's friendships with other children.
19.7 Influence related to awareness of Israel due to the school.
18.8 Influence related to helping children with homework.
18.0 Influence related to children who want to go to the synagogue.
16.4 Influence of adult friendships made through the school.
3.3   Influence related to Adult Education courses at school.

Norton table of maximum influence

%

34.6 Influence related to children's religious activity at home.
23.1 Influence due to a wish to support the ethos of the school.
23.1 Influence related to attending school assemblies etc.
19.2 Influence related to children's conversation at home.
19.2 Influence related to children learning to speak Ivrit.
19.2 Influence related to Adult Education courses at school.
19.2 Influence related to helping children with homework.

11.5   Influence related to awareness of Israel due to school.

11.5   Influence of adult friendships made through the school.

7.7   Influence related to children who want to go to the synagogue.

7.7   Influence of children's friendships with other children.

Brook table of maximum influence

%

38.4 Influence related to children's religious activity at home.

36.0 Influence related to children's conversation at home.

26.7 Influence related to attending school assemblies etc.

22.1 Influence due to a wish to support the ethos of the school.

25.6 Influence related to awareness of Israel due to school.

22.1 Influence of children's friendships with other children.

19.7 Influence related to children learning to speak Ivrit.

22.1 Influence of adult friendships made through the school.

22.1 Influence caused by helping children with homework.

13.9 Influence caused by children who want to go to the synagogue.

3.5   Influence related to Adult Education courses at school.

The various reasons above formed the basic framework of my questions to parents during the in-depth interviews. A leading question at every interview was: 'What do you feel is the main cause of the increase in the level of your religious observance?'

There were three main reasons given by parents that created the foundations of the increase in the parents' levels of religious observance.

- Firstly, there was the joy and satisfaction of the parents when they observed the Jewish knowledge of their children.

- Secondly, the above factor brought home to many parents the realisation and the understanding of the importance of supporting the religious teaching of the school in order to avoid giving a mixed message to the children.

- Thirdly, it was abundantly clear from the great majority of the interviews that what had initially started purely because of the children had become a way of life for many parents.

The following excerpts from the interviews illustrate these reasons.

The joy and satisfaction of parents due to the Jewish knowledge of their children

'You see their faces at half past three, beaming from ear to ear. How can you not reinforce it at the home and make an exciting thing because of your child's face? You've just seen it and it's glowing and you want to do something to reinforce the happiness.' (138/99)

'I think that it gives young children quite a thrill when they can teach their parents something. There's almost no expression on a child's face like one he has when he or she teaches his or her parents something that they didn't know.' (141/99)

'We thoroughly enjoy listening to the kids. The amount of pleasure we get from hearing them bench or make Kiddush or whatever they do it gives us tremendous pleasure.' (144/99)

'It's really a great pleasure. It comes naturally. There is nothing strange to him. He is growing up with it which is wonderful. He doesn't feel threatened by it. He doesn't feel that he shouldn't be doing it.' (111/99)

'They come home with loads of little snippets, different things that they'll tell you about. Something somebody had told them, certain things that I never knew. I learned about the raven and the dove from the story of Noah. I didn't know that there were the two birds until tonight. Now I always know what the parasha is and when it's Rosh Chodesh. I mean I'd never have known any of those things.' (116/99)

'That was really nice, I thought, you know I thought well that's really nice that the kids know something that I'm not even aware of. So we come to a Shabbaton and suddenly the kids know it. That's great.' (118/98)

'It does bring tears to my eyes to see all those children daven so beautifully and it's all in Hebrew. I don't know how you explain that. Their understanding of the festivals is so much greater than mine was at that age. Oh it was wonderful. I mean you know, the nachas [pleasure] as a parent, wonderful, they can bench!!' (120/99)

'He does the Kiddush very nicely, All the Chaggim he knows, he knows exactly where to find it, he knows every page.' (142/99)

The importance of home–school support

'My ethos is that I try and back up what they are learning at school as best as I can with what I can physically do rather than doing nothing at all.' (101/98)

'I think it's us wanting to continue whatever the kids were learning and not wanting to give them conflicting messages. I couldn't read Hebrew, so I actually started on a one to one learning programme. I didn't want them to come home and say, "this is alef beis or whatever" and I wouldn't be able to sit with them and know what they were saying, so I actually did start to learn and learned very slowly.' (143/99)

'We didn't feel that they would benefit by learning one thing at school and seeing something else at home. We wanted to do things for our children. When they came back from school having learned about Shabbat or kashrut, we felt that we wanted to help them by doing these things at home as well.' (114/98)

'Each week we learn the parasha. I mean I certainly never knew this before. Now I know what happens because of the children because they come home with the sedra sheet. And they have to answer questions on it. But it's amazing because they learn very quickly. Rachel, the older one, if she's reading she'll say to me, "there's no point in you helping me because you can't". So I did one of those Hebrew courses to learn how to read Hebrew so that I could help the children.' (105/98)

It started for the benefit of the children, and had become a way of life for the parents

'The children would be horrified if we were to do anything different. They learn this at school and we feel that it is important to support them. Now it is a way of life for us, and there is no way now that we would change.' (123/99)

'We didn't choose the Jewish school because we wanted it to have an effect on our lives, but it has. We chose it because of the children. It wasn't any kind of deliberate move.' (112/98)

'The children would talk about the festivals when they came home from school. I would be made aware of what was coming, I must say that I don't always look at the diary, it would just happen upon me, but I would know from the children what's coming. It would bring it home in a very practical way. So you can't ignore it and you end up taking part in it in one way or another. So I think that it's this sort of spin-off that pulls you in as a parent. Suddenly you realise that you were actually taking part in it events that may be organised at the school that you go along to. And in that way you gradually get drawn in. And once you're part of it, you're part of it, so you are doing it. Part of the objective is that it is already happening and you didn't even realise it.' (108/99)

'What has influenced it? Oh I am sure the children. Had it not been for the children with Emma wanting to, for me to be able to relate to what she was doing, I think that's why I've changed, definitely.' (121/99)

'Almost everything that we do, we started doing because we wanted the children to feel comfortable about what they had learned. We had a real feeling of pride. I feel that I want to show them that we too are a family who live in the way that the school is teaching. And it's lovely for us. Now we couldn't live any other way. We weren't like that when we were first married. We lived in a non-religious way, we didn't know any better. But now we do and we want to continue.' (102/99)

'The kids have come as a good excuse for us actually to do more. They've made us do more. They've pushed us. Neither of us has actually said that we don't want to do more. We've just done it because we felt that we wanted to do it.' (126/99)

'It's changed me in that I do some things that I've never done before. Kashrut I've done because you wanted to do kashrut. I went to shul because of the children, none of that would have happened if it wasn't for the children. The school has given me my Jewish education. It made up for what I lacked as a child.' (128/98)

'When Robbie was at the school, he wanted us to do certain things. At that stage he didn't want us to ride on Shabbat and we were. And there were certain other things that he didn't want us to do and he just asked us nicely and we said well this is the way that we are living. And then Jake came along and he also wanted us to go along a certain path. So we decided that we were going to conduct ourselves along that path. We don't drive to shul, we walk. It's a big thing as we have a 45–50 minute walk. So it's kind of a big thing to go to shul.' (130/99)

'Going through the yearly cycle, we do get sucked into all the activities. Tu Bishvat was never a big deal. I didn't even know what it was as a teenager. That's a very happy occasion and the children always do something to decorate pictures, and plant a tree for Israel, so I became more aware of what that was. The Omer, I didn't know what the days were but they were obviously counting it. If you go to the school hall you are aware of what day of the Omer it is.' (133/99)

'We wanted our children to see that we were happy to live in a religious way. To begin with it was really only for the children, but after a while it became important for us too.' (135/99)

W: 'Well they are pushing and pushing and pushing and they are succeeding. There's no compromise any more. He has stopped us from going out.'

H: 'I don't think that you can put it down to him stopping us, I think that we are adults and we can do what we want, we have the car keys and we can do that. I think that it's something that we don't feel uncomfortable doing. In other words to my mind it is not a major sacrifice.' (115/99)

'I would probably not have done as much as I do now. Yes, he's definitely changed me. I have a lot more respect for the Chaggim and in a way for him. I feel that I want to do more especially for him whereas I might have felt that I don't want to do as much or really anything at all. So yes he has drawn me in a lot more. I will take him to shul, whereas before I probably wouldn't have gone. It's something that I suppose I've always wanted to do but I've always drawn back from doing and as he wants to, it's given me more of a reason to do it.' (102/99)

'I don't think that it was so much that she was influencing us or telling us what to do, or that we were reacting to our daughter. We were just moving as a family in that way. I mean I couldn't possibly go to work if the children were going to be off school and apart from anything else I didn't want to go to work.' (103/99)

'I would like to become even more religious. I would be quite happy to, but we've sort of found our middle of the road that both of us are happy with. But I would be happy to become Shomer Shabbat. I've gone probably more the other way than my husband and I think that's from school.' (126/99)

'I always sense that it is being orchestrated at school in a deliberate way with the teachers making a play of that and for the culmination of something that was initiated at school and ends in the festival. That's probably the biggest effect it's had on us.' (135/99)

'At key times we decided on policy decisions as a family unit. When David for example was three it became clear that he had to wear tsitsit and so my husband said, well I ought to wear them too and if we have any further sons they will also have to wear them. So *therefore that's a policy decision. Around the same time we took the view that we wanted a quiet Shabbat and therefore we stopped listening to radio and telly which was probably one of the most profound decisions because it just lifted outside influence from Shabbat.'* (116/99)

'It was only that the kids felt we should have a sukkah at home, because of what had been taught at school and they had been speaking about it so much. But to tell you the truth, now that I have it, I enjoy using it as well as in shul with the others.' (136/99)

In the previous two chapters I investigated the specific areas in which parents had increased their level of religious observance and the main reasons that prompted them to change their way of life. In the following chapter I will examine whether the personal attitudes of parents towards their children may have determined the extent to which they have been influenced by them regarding any increase in levels of religious observance.

Chapter 7

Parental attitudes towards their children's Jewish identification

In their responses to the final section of the questionnaire, the vast majority of parents in all three schools agreed:

- that parents should direct their children's beliefs by example

- that in order to benefit from Religious Education at school, parents should reflect the value and ethos of the school.

This was a clear indication of what might be expected during the interviews.

Question 15 below is the final question of the questionnaire and deals with the parental response if children wanted them to be more observant.

	R	N	B
We are religious No change	20.5%	19.2%	22.1%
We will all change	7.3%	0.0%	3.5%
We will compromise	67.2%	65.4%	62.8%
Child Yes Family No	4.1%	15.4%	10.5%
Not religious No change	0.9%	0.0%	1.1%

Quite predictably, the majority of the parents decided on the easier option of being willing to compromise. However, this theme was developed extensively during interviews with parents to determine exactly how much of a compromise would be realistic. The following excerpts from the interviews deal with this question.

In family (106/98) both the husband and wife realised the importance of clear parental direction.

> H: *'Because I think you have got to start off with a certain point. You have got to try and show them what is correct and then they will come to their own conclusions when they get older. If you don't give them a grounding when they are younger, it's the same with other things. You've got to show children the right way.'*

> W: *'I think that they are too young at this stage to make a decision themselves. Children are very much influenced by their parents and they do tend to put their parents on a pedestal and they do accept at face value what you say. So if you don't make the decisions for them at this stage in life, then they stand no chance later on. Whereas I'd rather know that I've instilled certain barriers in them and accept that when they do get to teenage years it will be a natural rebellious stage against it which is fine. As long as they have had these values instilled in them in the hope that they will come back to them in later life.'*

They were, nevertheless, aware of the limitation of their own religious knowledge:

> H: *'One thing I knew that we did worry about. I knew that we were very middle of the road and I wouldn't be able to give them that background if I didn't send them to a Jewish school. I personally couldn't give them everything that they have got from a Jewish school because I'm not so observant.'*

They knew that eventually their children would enter a more rebellious stage.

H: 'I think that you have to lay down certain rules. There must be a point when they are no longer under your jurisdiction. When they are going out in the evening you can't dictate exactly what they are going to eat or drink. You have to trust them. If they decide to do their own thing, well that's up to them. You can say that whilst you are in our house you do it our way. I think that we would have to compromise somewhere along the line. We accept that rebellion is a natural thing.'

The wife replied instantly:

'I can't believe that. I don't know how I would cope with that. I think that the kashrut thing would be very traumatic in this house. The way I would respond is to explain that I see this as the way that Judaism will be able to carry on and I would see that as the beginning of marrying out. And that's the bottom line. I would be devastated if my children married out.'

Family (109/98) felt that they were directing their children's religious behaviour by example.

W: 'There's not much you can do about it. You just hope that by pointing them in the right direction and explaining it to them. You know that they will realise what they should or shouldn't do.'

They realised, however, that the time may come when the children would rebel against these parental norms which they viewed as a normal factor of the teenage years.

W: 'But more than that I think, and it might not do them any harm to have a go off the rails for a while as long as they realise what's going on. And that we keep the same here all the time at home, so that you know, because once they start saying that they can't do that and we start falling out with them, then that's it because you know that they are not going to come back. I think that you've got to have a considerable degree of tolerance. But let it be known that you are not happy about it.'

The wife stressed the need for tolerance towards the children in order to avoid any serious confrontation that could alienate them, but her husband was not too sure about this.

H: 'But in certain things, hopefully we will still be able to put our foot down.'

W: 'I don't think that there's going to be much that you can put your foot down for when they are fourteen or fifteen and they are out of the house.'

H: 'Yes, but no way if she wants to go out on a Friday night, what are you going to say?'

W: 'I always thought that will come up at some point. But how on earth are you going to stop them? How could you stop them?'

H: 'I can't lock her in but I mean we can make it clear what we feel can't we? And she knows that there isn't any negotiation taking place.'

The wife was still quite convinced that the policy of avoiding confrontation by offering a viable alternative was the best route to take.

'Well actually there will be enough going on, on a Saturday night but she'll want to go out on a Friday night, and you see that's the whole thing because if all her friends if she's got the right circle of friends who are going out to the Jewish youth club on a Wednesday and are meeting up on a Shabbat afternoon and are going out on a Saturday night, what on earth is she going to want to go out on a Friday night for? Unless it's to go out to somebody else's house, which isn't a problem. You see so there's a lot of things building up to that, it's not that she's going to come home now and say that because one of her friends do it she's not going to do it. You know that, and although I don't say no, you can't see that friend or you can't see that friend there are friends we can discourage without her realising it that they are being discouraged along the way. So hopefully it will be determined.'

Family (119/98) were asked about the extent that parents should direct their children's beliefs by example.

> H: *'That sounds to be important in so far as they reach an age when they begin to comprehend what it is all about. You have to show them by example and they will find that it reflects the school. She is still young for some things and doesn't yet realise why. It is important to be able to explain the why and wherefore although there are some things that are just done and that's it. So yes I think that is a true statement.'*

But when asked how they would react if their children eventually decided that they did not wish to be involved in a Jewish way of life, the wife replied:

> *'In my home they have to respect my wishes and if I turn fully kosher then they will have to abide by that in the house. What they do outside the house is up to them, providing that they don't eat bacon or ham, which we as a family do not eat.'*

The husband, however, appeared to be far more tolerant:

> *'Oh yes, I would be very happy, yes absolutely. As long as they weren't doing something that would be a detriment to themselves being silly, because unfortunately nowadays they've only got to watch out on the academic front, they need a good kick start in their adult formative years of 18 to 21.'*

Family (129/98) admitted that they were not observant and felt that to a certain extent their children should be allowed to make up their own minds about the level of religious observance that they wish to follow. It was evident that whatever this family did, in a religious sense, appeared to be purely at the request of their child.

> W: *'I want her to have the right start and make up her mind. If she said to me, I don't want to go shul on Simchat Torah, I would never disagree with her. I would never make her do it. At the moment she wants to do everything, because she's learning all about it at school, because she's going to shul. She sees the*

people she knows. She wants to do it, so I'm directing her. I'm not directing her beliefs, I'm directing her knowledge. I want her to know what every festival is. I want her to know where she comes from. I want her to know what her history is. I don't think that I really want to direct her beliefs. I'm not encouraging her to believe in God. The school's doing that for me. I don't have to do that. But if she said to me, of course there is, I think that I would let her make up her own mind. She is a little bit young. It's difficult for me as I've not encountered it really.'

I asked her whether by not giving a clear direction to her daughter, she is actually in another sense giving her some direction by allowing her daughter to develop in ways that might not be the right way. She replied: *'I think that you could be right. But I suppose that we've found our own levels.'*

She then stated that her child always watched her light the Sabbath candles on a Friday night. When I asked why she lit these candles, her response was very revealing.

'I don't know. I grew up with it. Obviously if we are going out to dinner to my brothers or somewhere else I don't light candles and leave them in the house alone. But I'm doing it for her. I'm trying to recreate the upbringing that I had, probably because I was happy with it. I never questioned it. I loved it and I am trying to do for my daughter what my mum did for me.'

There was another important reason which related to the importance of the family meeting and eating together on one special night of the week.

'But I think that's the one night that we try to eat as a family. On other nights, eating as a family with toddlers is horrendous: they throw food everywhere, really messy. We want them to go to bed so we can just relax. But Friday night we really try to do something together, with my mum as well. She was recently widowed and we try to be all together. We try to make it a family evening on a Friday night. But that's about as far as it goes.'

It was also interesting to learn how this family observed the festival of Chanukah in spite of building work being carried out in the home.

> *'Every Chanukah the candles come out and she enjoys it. This Chanukah we were having some building work, we had burst pipes, there was water dripping everywhere. It was an absolute nightmare and we had this chanukiah stood on this table here. There was a table in the middle of the room here, a hundred bricks in the corner, six doors, an outside door and a cement mixer and the chanukiah in the middle of the room but we did it. She could see that we were doing something.'*

Family (131/99) said that they were now living in a more observant manner than they were before they had children. They had decided to bring up their children to follow a more observant lifestyle.

> H: *'I've wavered when I was a student, I won't deny that and Deborah has as well before we had children. But we knew exactly the way we wanted to bring them up.'*

The husband did not see this as a practical form of guidance in what he termed a 'dictatorial' manner.

> H: *'They live in our environment. It's not just a matter of guiding them.'*

> W: *'Well it is guiding.'*

> H: *'Well, they're living with it, it's not guiding. You have to show them. It's not at all dictatorial. It's just that what they get at school they get here. You can't count going to school and learning about kashrut and then coming home and eating a pork chop. It just doesn't work. So the way they are at school is the way we are at home.'*

I asked them how they would feel if the children did not want to follow these ways as they grew older. The husband replied:

'I don't think that there is any problem at all. We can only do what we believe is right. They have got to choose their path in life and be happy with it. We certainly wouldn't fall out over it. I think that we would discuss it with them, but it has to be their choice.'

They were asked whether, as most of the families at the school were not observant, they ever had to compromise on their standards of religious observance, for example in respect of kashrut at children's parties.

W: *'Well, yes. If we were in London there was never a question of if you send your child to a Jewish school they would keep kashrut, and that is the problem with this school. There are definitely people who have parties who you do have to ask. And if they don't keep kosher then I make it very clear that our children can't eat there.'*

H: *'But there is no question of us lowering our standards.'*

According to his wife, the husband of family (127/99), who was not present at the interview, was totally non-observant. She stated that he was content for her to bring up the children in the way that she preferred. She said that if it were not for her work commitment she would take them to the synagogue on the festivals. When asked if the children would like her to take them, she replied:

'Yes, they probably would, but I know that I've never thought about the effect on them. It's never been an issue and probably won't be. We were lucky that last year all the festivals fell on a weekend.'

She accepted that her children were receiving a mixed message in relation to their religious observance but insisted that she and her husband did discuss all the things that the children would do and see.

'Yes, all the things that we do are always discussed. A lot of our friends keep very little and some keep more than us, and I know that some keep more because they've got children who are older and it's going to happen to us.'

When asked how she would feel if her children decided that they did not want to lead an Orthodox life but be more like their father, she replied:

'I do think that until they reach the age when they are going to make their own decisions about how they want to live, they will do as I say. I just hope that they will know what's right and what's wrong and I wouldn't stop them. I hope that they will realise what is the right thing to do. But in the end it will be up to them.'

The parents of family (132/99) were asked to comment on the importance of the family supporting the religious ethos and values of the school.

H: *'For Stephen, I think that he is being supported in whichever way we felt he could be supported, yes maybe, he is being well supported in doing it. He does a few things which probably I wouldn't do and he doesn't feel threatened by it, he doesn't feel that he shouldn't be doing it.'*

W: *'I think that because of the way that he learned it, it's a very nice way of doing it, he doesn't come up and say "Mum you must do it". It's a matter of how he learns it at school and whatever we do here and however we do it, you know, it's not as if we are not doing it at all. I feel that if we didn't make kiddush on Shabbat he would say that that would be really strange or if I didn't light the candles, but we are generally going hand in hand so it's not so confusing. It's very important because the school is doing it gently.'*

They were then asked to comment on whether parents of children of primary school age should direct their children's religious beliefs by example and practice and not let the children make up their own minds.

W: *'I think that at this stage it is very difficult. In certain areas you can direct and in others you must let them make up their mind. I don't want my child to be not religious at all on the other hand I don't want him to be too religious so that we can't cope with it or he can't live without it. You know I've got a friend who went to a very Orthodox school and became very very religious and now she doesn't even go to her parents' house. So they have had to turn their home life upside down. In our case, I mean me personally I feel that that is a bit too extreme, although it seemed to have worked for her.'*

Family (137/99) viewed their children's Jewish primary school education as being mutually advantageous, as a 'two-way thing'. These parents saw themselves as:

'Supporting the school, being involved with the school, being involved with the education, both secular and religious and supporting it.'

They were aware that they would also benefit.

'We knew that it would be reciprocated by virtue of when the children came home they would want to impart their knowledge they had, and it's just a kind of an all-round bonding thing.'

They admitted that they were genuinely interested in learning from their children.

'Not patronising the child but actually saying, I want to know, I don't really know, so what exactly did happen? I think the value of that is absolutely immeasurable. We know Maths and English and Reasoning and we can teach the kids that but if we don't know anything and the kids come back and teach it, that's terrific.'

Not only did these parents experience *'a great sense of pride'* in what their children were saying but they were also aware of another important aspect – a deeper awareness of Jewish identity.

'The fact they are talking about something which could affect how they are going to turn out is absolutely critical and you understand that they are learning all about what they are, it's about themselves as people, their religion, where they come from, it gives them a sense of identity.'

They felt that they were able to cope with the increased level of religious observance that their children were experiencing at the school.

> *'It seemed to be a level of religion we felt comfortable with. It was above our "then" level of religion and we felt comfortable supporting that. I don't think that we will have any regrets at the way we have gone. I don't think that we would have done things differently.'*

They were prepared to support the religious standards at the school in a sincere, open and honest manner.

> *'I think that we tried not just to give the boys a sense of well this is how we do things and this is how you do things, but we took cognisance of what they said and what they wanted.'*

It was clear, however, that the husband was determined to impart a sense of total honesty and integrity into his children.

> *'I've always been acutely aware, the real thing with me is the hypocrisy of conforming and really being "religious" and I'm very very conscious of the nonsense of how one can disturb a child's mind by saying, "well it's great that you learn this at school but we are not going to do it at home". I think that creates a very particular problem in a child's mind – such as where it gives them a sense of how to get out of situations and how to really evade responsibility. To me, my big thing is to cut out hypocrisy. I think that the whole environment reflecting the ethos of the school has always been honesty above all else, even if its meant saying, look I'm going to work today, I'm really sorry, I completely forgot that it was a Jewish holiday, as happened to me probably two months ago, I think it was Shavuot, two days and I had only put down one day and I am very careful, I've got a Jewish calendar at home and at work but I only put down one day and the second day I had a meeting. L would say to me yes you could miss it but I decided not to and I went to work and I said look I'm sorry I'm going, it's just a decision that I made. And it's honest, it may have been wrong and maybe that's not the ethos of the school because we are not quite conforming to what the school wants. But by me, honesty overrides that. And my view is yes they are right, I shouldn't have gone to work is my concession to them and in future I will avoid doing that.'*

Family (145/99) were already reasonably observant and were determined to support the religious ethos of the school in order to avoid the problem of confusion in the minds of the children.

> H: *'If you are going to send a child to a Jewish school and the kid is learning one thing at school, you have to, when he comes home, support what he is learning. If you don't support what is learned at school then you are confusing the child. I think that it is how we have got to bring our children up, believing in the principles behind the religious side of the school and whatever they learn at school is something that they should be seeing at home or bringing home to us.'*

He felt that it was important for the children to feel that what they are learning at school can also be applied at home and added that a two-way relationship with the school was important:

> *'Who knows, maybe I'll do something wrong, I only had a basic Jewish education, and they might say no, this isn't how we do it at school. Fine, I'll say, let's do it your way.*
>
> *I think that it is very important that if they are bringing it home, they are taking something from the school to the home and from the home to the school. You just hope that you can instil values into them and that the school can instil that as well.'*

His wife stressed the importance of the home providing the feeling and atmosphere of the Sabbath or festivals.

> *'But you know, when we are talking about ethos, a general feeling doesn't necessarily mean that we have to do everything straight down the line. As long as the feeling is there. So that on Pesach when they come home that there is a special feeling in the house, they know that we are changing over. It might not be the same way that the Rabbi does it but there is a feeling in the house. On Yom Tov they know that something exciting is happening. They are getting it from school and they know that there is something in the home as well.'*

She was especially sensitive to the sense of excitement brought home from school by the children.

> *'They thrive on the religious side of that school. On Yom Tov and Shabbat, everything, you know, the excitement they just bring to the front door with them. To me that is more precious than anything.'*

According to the husband, the school can claim success on two counts:

> *'If the child can change the parents or the child continues it on where he didn't come from an Orthodox background, that's where the school has really won. The school has instilled a way of life in the child that he never came from.'*

His wife commented about the possible attitude of some children towards their parents.

> *'I do also feel very strongly that I don't think the child should make the parents feel badly what they are doing, I think that is really important.'*

The parents of family (143/99) were asked to comment on whether parents should direct their children's religious observance or let them make up their own minds. The following excerpt is rather long but worth including in its totality.

> W: *'Both. I do feel both. I think that when they are younger you have to tell them what to do. You can't say to a six year old, "you decide whether or not to go to shul on Shabbat", or "you decide whether or not you're going to eat bacon". You can't give a child of six that freedom of choice. I think that you have to know the ground rules and you have to say what you will and won't do with a young child. And going I suppose on the maturity of the child you'll come to a certain point when you'll say, OK they are old enough now to start to make a few decisions for themselves, which is exactly what we did. We stopped forcing them to go to shul on a Yom Tov when they got to post Bar Mitzvah age, and we started to say to them, "look, what you want to do now,*

is your own life", to a certain extent. Of course you've got to conform to certain family values. We gave them a much freer rein when they started to become teenagers didn't we? Because I think that if you try to tie your children too much to you, it will have totally the opposite effect and they will just do what they want and just rebel. I know that's what I did. I went off shul and I went off religion totally as a young teenager. I just think that's one of the main reasons why we sent them to a Jewish school. It gives them the freedom of choice. They've got the knowledge, they've got the background and they can loosen the apron strings and then they can start to make their own decisions. You [to husband] you were totally totally anti-religious for years during your teenage years. I'm not saying you're a religious person now but you are much more aware of other people's observances and much more tolerant and you've been influenced again. I think that freedom of choice is very important but not when they are really young. When they are really young they must be under your guidance.'

H: *'Unless you've learned about something first, you can't make an informed choice. And that goes for a background of religious knowledge.'*

Family (104/98) felt that through their observant lifestyle they were showing their son the way they would like him to continue.

'Well it's how we want him to grow up. If we don't show him the way how is he going to find it? When he becomes eighteen he might say that he wants to be a Muslim or Catholic or whatever. I'd be disappointed when I think that we've given him the chance to choose a Jewish life for himself. If I don't show him the Jewish life how is he going to choose it?'

Conclusions from the above data, relating to the attitude of the parents towards their children regarding religious observance

The questionnaire data above indicated the high percentage of parents who felt that parents should direct their children's beliefs by example and not allow them to 'make up their own minds' in the early years. Only one family felt that children should be allowed to make up their own minds about whether to live in an observant manner or not.

A high percentage of questionnaire responses from parents who saw their role as influencing the children through example is very revealing. Bearing in mind the fact that the majority of these parents confirmed that their own level of religious observance had increased because of the influence of their children and the school, it was clear that they saw themselves as promoting a more religiously observant life style.

Many examples have been given in the chapter above of the comments made by parents, such as: *'You've got to show children the right way'; 'Children are very much influenced by their parents'; 'So if you don't make the decisions for them at this stage in life then they stand no chance later on.'*

An equally high percentage of responses from parents in respect of the second statement showed the value they placed on the importance of a mutual role between parents and the school in order to promote a higher level of religious observance. Most did not see a religious school as a threat which might intrude into their own private lives. It was apparent that the parents who were more 'traditional' than 'observant' felt the need to ensure a pleasant 'Jewish' family atmosphere for the children to enjoy. As one parent said, *'With such a family atmosphere at home, what on earth is she going to want to go out on a Friday night for?'* Another parent focused on the social family atmosphere of a Friday night meal: *'But I think that's the one night that we try to eat as a family ... Friday night we really try to do something together, with my mum as well.'*

The overall response from the returned questionnaires and the interviews focusing on the importance of a Jewish school was very favourable. One of the above comments appears to reflect the attitudes of many parents: *'They thrive on the religious side of that school. On Yom Tov and Shabbat, everything, you know, the excitement they just bring to the front door with them. To me that is more precious than anything.'*

The responses from the questionnaires, and even more so from the interviews, indicate that the great majority of the parents had increased their levels of religious observance due to the direct or indirect influence of their children and the school. But what was their real motive? Did the parents do so solely for the benefit of their children or intrinsically for themselves? This important question will be examined in the next chapter.

Chapter 8

Sincerity of intention

To what extent have parents of the children actively embraced a religious life-style **for its own sake** and, conversely, to what extent have parents overtly increased their level of religious observance purely **for the benefit of their children** or when their children are with them?

I have already referred to previous research particularly in the USA which showed that 'regardless of having attended a Jewish day school, there appears to be only a minimal adult identification with Jewish religious life in later years'. Also that 'evidence showed that it was only when the parents and their home life had supported the religious ethos and teaching in the school that the pupils continued to identify in later years with Jewish religious life'. I added, 'if it can be shown that Jewish day schools do have an influence … it would suggest that these pupils will be more likely to continue to identify in their adult years in a … Jewish religious manner'.

Based on the above data, it is clear that, to a greater or lesser extent, all the families increased their level of religious observance due to the influence of their children. It is likely that any such increase may also have been due to the wish of parents to support the religious teaching of the school in order to ensure maximum benefit for their children.

Some of the following excerpts from interviews have already been included as a part of previous chapters but have been repeated here in order to focus on what might be termed the 'real motives' of the parents.

I would now like to examine the comments of families whose overall level of religious observance had initially increased due to the wish to support their children. They subsequently became personally observant in their own religious lives.

A good example can be seen in the comments of the husband and wife of family (135/99) who admitted to being non-religious when they were first married but decided to send their children to a Jewish primary school. They felt that it would be beneficial to the children if they saw that their parents supported the religious ethos of the school. They subsequently discovered that it was to have an effect not only on their own level of observance but also on their overall attitude to Judaism.

> *'To begin with it was really only for the children, but after a while it became important for us too.'*

In a practical sense this resulted in their own personal involvement with synagogue life.

> *'I knew that at school they were learning about Shabbat and going to shul and I felt that it would be sensible if I took them there for the children's service, but after a while I got used to going and I enjoyed being there myself. When we moved, we wanted to live near the synagogue for the sake of the children and ourselves. We now go regularly.'*

It was evident that these parents were prepared to go even further should their children request it:

> *'We are always ready to learn and to do more things if the children feel that it is important or if we feel it is important ... There must be a knock-on effect of the children becoming more observant and saying, we don't want to do this on Shabbat, and we shouldn't be doing this ... But I think that it's something that we don't feel uncomfortable doing. In other words to my mind it is not a major sacrifice not going out for a few months in the summer and on Shabbat I'm kind of torn between it. But we might be able to tolerate it. We try not to be confrontational or defensive without reason. It's not easy.'*

Another example of a major change in their family life was greater observance of the Jewish dietary laws.

'The children always seem to know what they may eat or not eat. They have learned about these things at school and they want to keep these laws at home. They are very careful especially when other people offer them food and this has also made it important for us to do the same as far as is possible.'

I noted in an earlier chapter that greater observance of the festivals, especially in synagogue attendance, required a higher degree of extra commitment from working parents who had to take time off from their regular employment. This was certainly the case with the husband of the above family.

'I think that probably the greatest area that's had an effect has been on me going to shul on certain holidays where I or we might not have gone. Say Sukkot or not the major holidays but the other holidays, that's prompted us again when they say that there has been some build-up at school.'

It is likely that the following comment he made will be understood and appreciated by teachers in many Jewish schools.

'I always sense that it is being orchestrated at school in a deliberate way with the teachers making a play of that and for the culmination of something that was initiated at school and ends in the festival. That's probably the biggest effect it's had on us.'

With family (129/98), it was helping their daughter with her school homework that provided the impetus.

'Our daughter came home from school and said that she had to do a project on kashrut and she asked us to help her with it. We all got involved. It was then that we realised that this was for real. What we do at home we must do when we eat out.'

For family (102/99), the influence of the children was a catalyst towards greater personal observance of the parents.

'They love teaching us all the Shabbat songs they learn at school. We stopped having the TV on Shabbat and made a proper Shabbat atmosphere for them because it seems that it is the way they enjoy and so do we. Now we couldn't live any other way. We weren't like that when we were first married. We lived in a non-religious way, we didn't know any better. But now we do and we want to continue.'

Family (110/99) were not initially observant but made an early decision to support the religious ethos of the Jewish school attended by their children.

'Definitely, it's all for the children ... We didn't want to put them into that position where they are learning one thing at school and they come home and we say, "Forget what you learned at school". So what the school is teaching them, we want them to come home and have the same values. If I can help to make them feel happy about what they are learning and what they are doing, I will ... We stopped using the phone on Shabbat. I have actually found it harder than I thought I would. It was a very drastic change for me. We made a decision and we just did it. But it was the children who were saying that you shouldn't press buttons on Shabbat.'

Family (104/98) were not observant when they first married but it was very clear that they had made considerable changes from the days when there was just the two of them and Friday nights were no different to any other night of the week. The husband was quite sure where the impetus had come from.

'When we got married we kept a kosher home, but that's basically all that we did. And I honestly believe that subconsciously we both probably felt that we should do a bit more and the kids have come as a good excuse for us actually to do more. They've made us do more. They've pushed us. Neither of us has actually said, no we don't want to do more. We've just done it because we felt that we wanted to do it. It gives you a reason for doing it.'

His wife echoed her husband's views.

> *'I would say that the children played a huge part in it. Certainly now Shabbat is Shabbat. On a Friday night I light the candles, the children light candles, we make kiddush, we have a nice dinner. But when there was just the two of us, I don't think there was any difference to any other night of the week ... We would be quite happy to become even more religious but we've sort of found our middle of the road that both of us are happy with. I think that's from their school. Just trying to back up what they do at school.'*

But how far would they be prepared to go? The following dialogue is very revealing.

> H: *'I'm quite comfortable with what we do now. I don't particularly want to go any further. I'm quite comfortable as we are now.'*

> W: *'My ethos is that I try and back up what they are learning at school as best as I can with what I can physically do rather than doing nothing at all. But I will only go so far.'*

It seemed that this was particularly true in regard to the dietary laws where kashrut observance out of the home was not so strict.

> H: *'We would probably explain to her why we do what we do, which is keeping a kosher home but eating out in restaurants because that's not in our home but we feel comfortable doing it. I guess we would try to ascertain how strongly she felt about it. If she felt particularly strongly about it, then maybe we would go with what she wanted.'*

> W: *'I don't know. I don't agree. I think that we would stick to what we normally do.'*

Although she admitted that there was a limit to the extent of their level of religious observance, they made far greater effort to observe the festivals properly in their efforts to support at home what their children were learning at school.

'We make more effort. I think the point is we will make more effort when it comes to whatever festival it is.'

The following excerpts from other interviews are examples of the majority of the parents whose personal level of religious observance had increased purely for the purpose of wishing to support their children's school experiences. It was evident that this was the primary reason and not because the parents felt that they personally wished to live in a religiously observant manner.

Family (140/99) is of particular interest because of the differing backgrounds of the husband and wife. The wife came from a totally non-observant secular Jewish American family whilst her husband, who had grown up as a part of an ultra-Orthodox Sephardi family, had become an 'anti-religion rebel'. He admitted that he had discarded all the outer trappings of any semblance to a religious life, whereas she had never experienced anything other than a minimal identification with a basic Jewish way of life. What was abundantly clear was the current involvement of the whole family in what can be termed 'a Jewish way of life'. However, it was equally clear that everything was being done purely to support the wishes of their three children.

Even though she was unable to read Hebrew and felt like *'a fish out of water',* the wife began taking the children to the synagogue on a Shabbat purely because *'they wanted to go'.* She initially viewed Shabbat as *'a nice night to have the family together. Not as a religious thing but it's a nice time for the five of us for that reason to sit down and have dinner. So that would be something as they get older that we would still keep. It would be some kind of continuity.'*

She spoke of her increased knowledge of the Jewish festivals due to the children and made mention of one particular Pesach. *'That was the one time in my life where I actually remember all of them making a stand there.'* The children had insisted on a full and thorough festival preparation in the home and the parents agreed. She added, however, *'because it was at an acceptable level we did it. It's only when it goes to another level that it's not acceptable.'*

They were pleased that their children were receiving a Jewish education from the school, but take note of her words: *'We enforced it as much as we can and we want to … but in our home we will do as we see fit.'*

91

In the majority of families interviewed, it was evident that even if the husband and wife each had differing attitudes to religious observance, as was occasionally the case, they generally appeared to be united when encouraging or setting an example for their children.

This was not the case, however, with family (120/99) where the husband was relatively unobservant and did not hide this from his wife and daughters who were becoming more religiously observant. This situation was being faced in a realistic manner by the wife who was determined to support and encourage her children's religious observance. *'Before we had children we already decided that they were going to be brought up how I wanted from the religious point of view. I think that if it wasn't for my input it wouldn't happen.'*

This was certainly the case with regard to synagogue attendance on Shabbat.

> *'At the moment it's only me doing it but eventually he'll come because the children are driving him mad. I can see that will happen. But it probably won't happen until she gets to an age when she can manage to go. He's going to have to go one day when she is Bat Mitzvah.'*

But it was clear that she anticipated a future change in her husband's level of observance due to the pressure of her daughter.

> *'I'm waiting for her to point out that her father eats certain things out that we don't at home and say to him, "you shouldn't be eating that". She probably will but she's not done it yet. I think that he'd expect it. I think that he's just waiting for that to happen.'*

I asked them how they would respond if their child wanted to observe the Sabbath more fully. The wife replied:

> *'It depends what it is. It depends how much she is going to change. If she came home from shul and said that she wanted to go to shul every Shabbat then we would try to tolerate that. If there are other things that she came home with and said that she wanted to do, well it really depends. The only thing that I think that the school did do was to increase their awareness and that if they really wanted to do something that they have learned that we do not do, then it*

will probably be accommodated. We already have changed in that we try to go to shul on festivals, all the additional festivals that we didn't keep at all. The whole time we were married until the last couple of years we had not kept them at all. I mean I knew they were occurring but it didn't have any impact on my life at all. Because she is learning about it at school and in that sort of environment, she should be aware of what she is supposed to do.'

Family (139/99) were generally non-observant but occasionally took their children to synagogue on a Shabbat morning.

'Yes, it's always difficult. I mean some Saturdays we do take the children to shul and then it's always the question of how far do we go? I'm happy for the children to have friends to play to make that a day that's different. I don't like to go shopping on a Saturday, I'm just happy to have a lazy day. My parents like to come round and if the children stay here they can have friends here to play. So that's different, whereas I suppose that before we had children we would go anywhere. We went shopping.'

The wife of family (139/99) had normally been at work on festival days, but one year the Easter holidays coincided with Pesach. Although her husband was at work she decided to take her children to the synagogue. The results were not what she had anticipated.

'I must say that I had an awful time because my particular circle of friends are often at work. I had some of the kids back here to play. The children were OK but I was bored out of my mind. I couldn't stand it, I couldn't do my normal thing after going to shul and coming home. I felt so isolated. I'm not from a religious circle. It's great if you are. I thought I can't do this because there isn't a big enough family. It is very lonely if you are on your own. I think that after that, that was when I stopped pushing to become more religious. I thought this isn't going to be very practical. It's rather sad really actually, you know, after having looked forward to it so much, and then I thought I'm not happy.

But now I realise that it's not practical because I haven't got family like with friends who are interested enough to do this and they have a family or circle of friends who are interested enough and they all get together and they are socialising. You have to do that on a Yom Tov or you would go out of your mind with boredom. Unless you have been to shul – that's it. It's a very long day if it's only you and the children and you can't do anything else.'

The absence of like-minded friends is a crucial factor. It is, without doubt, a great bonus for any family who wish to increase their level of religious observance if their family and friends are like-minded. In the above case, there seemed to be no other social or family group with whom to share the experience. This is the reason why the husband felt that any increase in the religious life of the above family was like 'a chasm' that could not be crossed.

'It's a big jump to do this when you've been doing what we're doing now and then to become Shabbat observant. For me it's like a chasm, I can't really cope with that. I know that my wife considered it very seriously.'

Family (134/99) admitted to being unobservant Jews but nevertheless felt that it was important to transmit to their children a sense of pride in their religion.

'We can never hide from being Jewish. We will stand up to be counted with the rest so they might as well know and enjoy who they are.'

They said that they were willing to increase their level of observance although it was very clear that any changes were unlikely to be major.

'We have started to do more. If they are not too tired we have started to do kiddush on a Friday night and he understands it and he likes it. We take the children to the synagogue on Yom Tov but very rarely on a Shabbat.'

But they were certain that any increase in their religious observance, however slight, had been due to the influence of their children.

'We are more kosher. The menorah on Chanukah, we never did it before really except when we were kids ourselves and then it goes

away, and now it has come back again, lighting the candles. The seder has been important. Rosh Hashanah, Fridays and the holidays have always been important.'

However, when asked to what extent would they be prepared to follow any request from their children which would necessitate leading a more observant life, her reply was very revealing:

'We spoke about this. I said that if our son comes home and says that we should be kosher, I mean we've even got our degree of kosher, we don't bring pork in the house, you know it's really weird and it certainly wouldn't make the odds if we only ate non-kosher meat, no way.'

It was at this point that they made the following remark:

H: 'There's a little flame that keeps burning, maybe that's the important thing, there's a little flame somewhere ...'

W: 'that could be rekindled by Jonny.'

When asked about the possibility of their children wanting the family to be even more observant with increased synagogue attendance or observance of the dietary laws, her response appeared to centre around one main concept. In a practical sense she felt that she could cope with any request from the children.

'Maybe I'll turn round and say, Oh we don't do that here Jonny, don't worry about it because it's not important to us. Maybe that's what I'll do, I don't know.'

Nevertheless she did admit that there was a limit as to how observant she and her husband were prepared to be.

'I'd like to think that I would make it as comfortable for my children to be in that particular community, in that school, as much as possible for our home life. If he says that he wants to have kosher plates then we will do it, it's not such a big deal. If that's how he would feel happy for friends to come home and maybe not to see a

'non-kosher' Chicken Kiev in the fridge than that's fine by me for the period that he wants it. And if it goes on, I don't think that it will be so difficult. If he wanted to light candles or do something more, then we'd do it, wouldn't we?'

The final comment of the wife of the above family seemed to sum up her own real inner feelings and attitude to a more religious life.

'I'm terribly comfortable with what I do. I don't need to think about whether I've bought the right ingredients for the right meal. I don't have to feel guilty about that. There are other things to feel guilty about. I think that probably I should encourage them otherwise … perhaps they will lose it or I don't know, I don't think that I got anything from Jewish education that made me keep a kosher home and an observant home.'

One of the most interesting interviews was with family (141/99). The wife had a very clear reason for her religious observance, although there was a clearly defined limit regarding their level of observance. This is a woman with her own very strong personal attitude towards Judaism which was coupled strangely with her lack of belief in God. It was evident that she was doing her best, so that her child can *'see some connection between what she is learning at school and between what she sees at home'.* Although she had stated *'I'm not directing her beliefs, I'm directing her knowledge',* she also added that her child *'knows that Mummy doesn't believe that there is a God'.*

'She watches me light the candles on a Friday night. I'm doing it for her. I'm trying to recreate the upbringing that I had, probably because I was happy with it. I never questioned it. I loved it and I am trying to do for Miriam what my mum did for me. I believe that Miriam has to see some connection between what she is learning at school and between what she sees at home. I want her to have the right start and to make up her mind. I'm not directing her beliefs, I'm directing her knowledge. I'm not encouraging her to believe in God. The school's doing that for me. She knows that Mummy doesn't believe that there is a God, but that some people do and she's learning about it.

But she's learning that we're taking our own little segments of what she sees at school and then see them happen at home in a different way. I've tried very very hard to let her understand bits of what I believe. So we're kind of interpreting it in a different way. I will still maintain my beliefs but I will always accommodate the children to the best of my ability. So if they decide not to watch TV on Shabbat then I'll do my best to make sure that doesn't happen.'

They were not interested in going to the synagogue on the Sabbath although they were willing to allow the children's grandparents or others to take them.

'Never in a million years would my husband take the children to the synagogue. But he would arrange for someone else to do it. He's lost in a service. He feels lost there. He would say, "You go to shul and I'll clean the car." But I don't like to go either. The last time I sat through a service in shul was my own wedding. I couldn't do it. My in-laws go and they like it and they take the children.'

On Friday nights family (147/99) used the occasion for a family meal but pointed out: *'that's about as far as it goes'.*

'Friday is the one night that we try to eat as a family. Friday night we really try to do something together, with my mum as well. She was recently widowed and we try to be all together. And we try to do it here if it's with my mum, because it's easier if we do it together because I have to put them to bed. There is something in the home. We try to make it a family evening on a Friday night. But that's about as far as it goes. Throughout the year she can see little bits and pieces.'

It is interesting to note her comments when asked what her level of religious observance might have been if their child had not attended a Jewish school.

'It would have been different. I think I would have either played more of a part in the religion to give her that start or not doing it at all, and forget it. You know, we're just not religious at all. Had we have not lived here, I think that would have happened to us, not being a part of the Jewish community.'

Family (109/98) had certainly become more observant and were quite certain that this was entirely due to the influence of their young son. The husband admitted that his own attendance at the synagogue was for the sake of his son:

> *'I will take him to shul, whereas before I probably wouldn't have gone. It's something that I suppose I've always wanted to do but I've always drawn back from doing and as he wants to, it has given me more of a reason to do it.'*

It was also evident that other aspects of Jewish life were impinging on the whole family:

> *'I feel that I want to do a little bit more especially for him whereas I might have felt that I don't want to do as much or really anything at all. So, yes, he has drawn me in a lot more.'*

This included a stricter observance of the dietary laws not only at home but also when eating out.

> *'But now he knows that he doesn't go to places like that because they are not kosher. Yes, maybe there was a time when we would have gone but we definitely do not go now and there are no two ways about it.'*

The husband of family (118/98) clearly did not enjoy going to the synagogue although he admitted that as his daughter gets older he would be prepared to take her if she requests it, realising the need to support the studies of his children.

> H: *'I've only been a few times, dare I say under sufferance. But I can see that's sort of changing. Judy is very curious and all her friends do.'*

> W: *'She's been a few times.'*

> ML: *'Would you go if Judy asked to go because her friends were going?'*

W: *'Yes, if we are pushed like that because I want to be more involved. The more I think about it, the more I want to be involved with it. I feel it's a community task. I mean I see my daughter go to a Jewish school and when she comes home she recites prayers and whatever and which I know that when she is going to study for her Bat Chayil and our son for his Bar Mitzvah, I don't want to be behind them, I want to be ahead of them so that I know what they are doing.'*

They admitted to being not entirely kosher at home but understood the potential social difficulty that it created.

'It does cause problems if her other friends who come round are coming from a fully kosher home and I've got to respect that. I've always got kosher food in the house and I never mix. I know that it's hypocritical when my utensils aren't fully kosher.'

However, the parents were involved in a school Shabbaton, which was a school-based family Shabbat experience. This may have been the catalyst which changed his attitude.

'We went to the school Shabbaton. We went as a family as a group, a family with all our friends. It was lovely to see the children in action and participating and it made me realise that I want to get involved.'

In their wish to support the religious ethos of the school, family (113/99) ensured that everything at home was fully kosher but when eating out they admitted that

'If the children are not with us, we are a bit more ambivalent.'

The influence of their children was especially impressed on the husband who appeared to have learned the rudiments of a seder from his children rather than from his parents.

'Pesach is the highlight of the Jewish academic year at school. It's beautifully done with a lot of seders and the children know all the songs so well. Because they know the songs so well, it seems a shame

not to give them the opportunity to repeat it. My husband never had proper seders. He never knew how to participate fully. But now we take it very seriously because the kids take it very seriously in school.'

In a similar manner, the wife of family (118/98) felt that their level of Pesach observance had increased due to their son who

'had a tremendous influence at Pesach time as that was all very important to him. How did I respond? I did it because that was what he wanted. When I grew up, Purim wasn't observed at all at my parents' house. But our children would dress up every year and it would make me conscious of the fact that it was happening, that it was a pleasant festival. So suddenly I'm interested in that, and in our own way we were beginning to take some part in observing it.'

Her husband, whose childhood had not been observant, stated that his knowledge and ultimate involvement in all the festivals were due to the children.

'The children would talk about the festivals when they came home from school. So you'd be, I would be made aware of what was coming.'

In another case, the wife of family (134/99) admitted that she experienced a religious dilemma regarding the festival of Pesach. Her own level of observance and belief was very low although she felt that she wanted her child to be aware of what was required.

'We had Pesach with the family at my mother-in-law's and my sister-in-law's houses so that she can enjoy what she is learning at school and then put it into practice. Just because I think that it's all rubbish, it doesn't mean that I want her to know that. Just at the moment it is important for her. There's no point in me sending her to a school when we're pretending it doesn't exist when she comes home. It does and people believe it. At Pesach there are things that I refuse to do. I refuse to buy Pesach washing up liquid and ketchup, and tea bags as a whole. I'll open a new box though. I will show her that I am doing something different. We do things in our own little way.'

This is certainly a difficult situation and a problem that the child will experience as the years pass. There are two interesting factors in the above example that are worthy of examination. Firstly, that the child had been sent to a Jewish school in order to learn about the Jewish way of life. Secondly, the feeling of the parents that they were prepared to join in the seder at the home of other members of the family, not merely because it was a social event and a family get-together, but *'so that she can enjoy what she is learning at school and then put it into practice'*. It seems that a major difficulty faced by this and other families who begin to become more observant is the social problem with existing family and friends. *'We would go as far as he wanted really, but our contemporaries, our friends are really not that religious at all.'*

The positive effect and involvement of the children during the family seder service on Pesach was a frequent comment made by parents. For family (115/99), their greatly improved and enjoyable seder was due *'to what the children have learned at school'*. They admitted with a sense of pride, *'all thanks to the school. It has really changed our lives.'* They felt that they wanted to impress on their children *'that we too are a family who live in the way that the school is teaching'*.

Some final thoughts on the data presented in this chapter

Parents who personally wished to live in a more observant manner gave the impression that there would be no limit to the possible future increase in their religious observance, for example, family (134/99) who stated quite clearly: *'We would go as far as he wanted really.'* However, with only one exception it was evident from a closer examination of their statements that certain specific limitations or problems might indeed occur.

But could they and would they increase their level of observance in social isolation? They referred to their contemporaries and friends who *'are really not that religious at all'*. This may well be an important problem for families such as these. The level of observance of family (137/99) had reached what they considered was: *'a level of religion we felt comfortable with'*. They admitted that this had been an increase compared to previous years *'and we felt comfortable supporting that'*, but they did not give me the impression that there would be an unlimited increase in the future.

Family (110/99) used the qualifying word 'if', when considering how important it was to support, in a practical manner, the religious teaching of the school. *'If I can help to make them feel happy about what they are learning and what they are doing, I will.'* This implies that there could be future occasions when the parents will consider the request and decide that they could not.

The wife of family (120/99) gave every indication that she wished to support and encourage their children in every way: *'anything that she wanted to do we'd never disagree'*. However, with the added problem of a relatively non-observant husband it was little wonder that she added later: *'I suppose that there is a lot more that we could and should be doing.'*

The above five parents, although initially giving a clear impression that they would unreservedly increase their own level of religious observance, clearly had already decided that there would still be certain restrictions and limitations. With only one family (135/99) was there a clear indication that they would indeed do everything in their power to support the requests of their children. What had started as a way of doing something for their children had ended with total family commitment: *'We wanted our children to see that we were happy to live in a religious way. To begin with it was really only for the children, but after a while it became important for us too.'*

Data from all the families interviewed has shown that the main reason for an increase in the parents' level of religious observance was for the benefit of their children who had made such requests. Although the majority of families had increased their level of religious observance, it was clearly more for the benefit of their children and focused primarily on the practical aspects of observance rather than the personal spiritual benefit they themselves received. There was usually a limit to such observance. In some cases it was shown that any such increase may also have been due to the wish of parents to support the religious teaching of the school in order to ensure maximum benefit for their children.

Amongst the noticeably smaller percentage of parents who had increased their observance more for their own sake, the majority stated that they were prepared and willing, without limit, to increase even more their own level of religious observance should their children make this request of them.

From the evidence of the questionnaires and the interviews, it was abundantly clear that, with very few exceptions, all the families whose level of religious observance had increased had admitted that it was due to the influence of their children and the school.

Chapter 9

How did the parents view their own anticipated future level of religious observance?

It is important to acknowledge that any accurate research is dependent upon what *has* taken place or *is* taking place at the moment of observation or interview. This cannot be the case in respect of what *might* take place in the future. It is speculative. However, in this specific area of research, I feel that such data still has much to offer. It can be seen as a clear indication which reflects the feelings of the parents relating to their attitude towards religious observance. It can also reflect the extent to which parents had increased their level of religious observance for the sake of their children or because they personally had become more observant for its own sake.

Section 1: The likely responses of parents if their children would ask them to increase their level of religious observance

Family (140/99) was very positive.

> *'I think that I would discuss it and see what they wanted us to do. I would take each individual thing on its merits and decide if I was capable of doing it and if I was interested in doing it. I would consider them very seriously and try my best to do it.'*

The husband of family (142/99) pointed out that he and his wife were prepared to live in a more observant manner even though most of their own personal friends were not at that level.

'We would go as far as he wanted really but we probably would take that step further if it meant that he could observe more what he wanted to observe more.'

The wife of family (102/99) had actually suggested to her husband that he should work on a Sunday rather than a Saturday. His response was certainly positive:

'Yes, it could possibly happen. I think we could cope with that. As far as levels of observance, everybody takes Shabbat or observing to their own level and I am quite happy taking it to that level.'

Similarly the wife of family (105/98) viewed the possibility of increased religious observance in a reasonably positive manner, stating that:

'Ten years ago I would never have believed what we are doing now.'

Family (115/99) had responded positively to the pressure of their children. It was ultimately the combined pressure of both of their sons that made the family decide to conduct their own lives in a more religiously observant manner.

'Well they are pushing and pushing and pushing and they are succeeding. We might be able to tolerate it. We try not to be confrontational or defensive without reason. It's not easy.'

Family (113/98) were asked how they would respond if their children wanted them to become even more observant. The opposing attitudes and responses of husband and wife were very revealing. The husband, who felt that they were already leading a religious life, had no doubt that they would be prepared to become even more observant, but his wife was not so sure. There was a limit to the extent of increased observance that the wife was prepared to undertake:

'It depends to what extent they want us to go. I will do anything for them but it will not change me that much.'

But when asked to what extent she would be prepared to increase her observance, she replied:

'I don't think that we'd go to that next stage. I would say to them, look, I've always said to you that we're doing what we can to do what we feel is the right level for us. And I am prepared. I would be prepared to do more within the home. I would be prepared to do whatever we're going to do.'

The wife of family (117/98) believed that her children fully understood how far their parents were prepared to go. Nevertheless she would be prepared to increase her level of observance if it would benefit her children.

'So say for instance if our daughter joined Bnei Akiva, during the winter I would walk to shul when I would bring her there and I would obviously walk back with her. I would make life easy for her. I would never say, no you're not doing that.'

There was a clear difference of opinion between husband and wife of family (129/98). The wife was prepared to increase her level of religious observance whereas her husband had certain reservations.

W: *'I could be persuaded to do a lot more.'*

H: *'Not me. What if they say don't drive your car on Shabbat. Would you do that?'*

W: *'Yes. If they said don't talk on the phone on Saturday, I wouldn't.'*

H: *'You wouldn't do it?'*

W: *'No, I wouldn't do it.'*

H: *'I would try to find a way to explain that I will back them up if they want to do it. I grew up differently from them and they will have to respect my way as I will respect their way. It's not easy to talk with children in this way. One of the problems of being in a Jewish school is the lack of knowledge about other religions. They know nothing about other things that can be very beautiful. They are lacking in information. Sometimes I have to find a way to explain to them that they are Jewish but here are some other things in the world. This is why I don't want them to go to a Jewish secondary school.'*

The husband of family (143/99) felt that they were already leading a religious life at a level that suited them. Any increase in that level was dependent on the effect it would have on them.

'I suppose that the answer is, it depends what. If they said that they wanted to go to shul every week and they wanted to walk, well maybe that's pushing it. If they wanted to go to shul more often, that isn't pushing it.'

The husband of family (104/98) felt that the whole family were *'moving together'* as a unit. *'I think that to be honest we are probably doing more than the school would demand, certainly more than the school would suggest.'*

But in contrast, the wife of family (145/99) felt that she would probably resist any effort by her children to live in an even more observant manner.

'I was going through a stage a few years ago of wearing a more modest dress attire, but really I didn't feel that comfortable. I was mixing maybe in frummer circles. And I don't like going to these separate seating larks.'

Both husband and wife of family (136/99), who were already observant regarding dietary laws, were in agreement that there was only one further main area in which they could increase their level of observance.

'The only thing would be our observance of Shabbat and the festivals and I think that would probably be it really.'

Family (139/99) said that they would consider any request from their daughter, as long as they felt that it would not be too much of an imposition on them, but, as with many other families, emphasised that it depended on exactly what their child wanted them to do.

In a similar way, the husband of family (110/99) was very positive regarding an increased level of observance due to the pressure of their children but it would be dependent on the level and the degree of additional observance that their children had asked them to reach.

'I think that there would have to be a limit. A lot would of course depend on what it was that they wanted us to do. Due to the children we have proper kiddush on Shabbat and sing Zemirot during the meal and bench. Due to the children we don't cook or drive on Shabbat. We have a time switch for the lights, we have a proper seder. We try to do most things but we are not extreme ultra religious. The children can be as religious as they like but we would limit how religious we want to be. Well we are doing so much now which all began because of our children so I suppose that doing more wouldn't be terrible if it helped to keep the family together as long as it was something that we could adapt to and cope with.'

The wife of family (141/99) was prepared to accommodate any increased level of observance for the children, but insisted that it would not have any long-term effect on her own personal level of observance.

'While they are living under my roof the home can remain kosher. I'll still get in my car on Shabbat and I will drive. I will still maintain my beliefs but I will accommodate the children to the best of my ability. So if they decide not to watch TV on Shabbat then I'll do my best to make sure that doesn't happen. I'm not really interested in time switches for lamps. I'm certainly not going to cut the toilet paper. But they can if they want to. If our children want to be more Orthodox then that's OK and I'm prepared to learn from them. But until somebody can convince me, my beliefs will remain the same. I am quite prepared to do whatever is necessary to make my children understand that whatever I believe and whatever they believe won't change.'

The response of the wife of family (133/99) was very similar to the above comment:

'I suppose that there is a lot more that we could and should be doing. I think that I've already pushed him a long way along the line,

probably as far as he is prepared to go. I suppose that we should go a bit further and shul on Shabbat is the next thing. It wouldn't mean that I would change my life style. It has happened to a couple of families I know. I do think that it gets to a point where it's fine and we would ensure that we will try and respect them but it wouldn't mean that we would be changing our life style. By that time they would be of an age to make their own decisions. I can't see us changing.'

Although the wife of family (125/98) considered that although she might be prepared to increase her level of religious observance at the request of her children, her response was not a very strong one. Her husband appeared to be more realistic in his response.

W: *'I might because the older one keeps saying to me there are other things and there are perfectly nice things and of course there are. And now delicatessen wise it's so easy to get nice Jewish food out that it might be easier to do. It becomes easier to do.'*

H: *'I try to make a stronger stand when I'm out. I don't always succeed. I'm not saying I'm perfect but particularly when I'm with the children I try to respect their ways. And I will try not to eat non-kosher, certainly if I'm with them. But I do lapse sometimes.'*

W: *'There was one holiday when we only ate fish all the time.'*

H: *'There are holidays when I only eat vegetarian. I try, I try but I'm not very observant. And I agree with the philosophy that we should encourage them to eat kosher food if possible. But none of us is perfect and we come from a background that isn't strictly Orthodox in that way.'*

W: *'And it's a great treat to go out and have a schnitzel or whatever.'*

H: *'My parents didn't even keep a kosher home. So I feel that I've moved forward a little bit. Not very far but I've moved a little bit.'*

An earlier comment made by family (134/99) referred to *'a little flame that keeps burning'*. Perhaps that is the important thing, that there is a little flame somewhere that could be rekindled by their young son. I feel that all the families who have been interviewed in this research project have indicated in one form or another that they have this 'little flame' of Jewish identity that keeps burning. With some families it is evident that the flame is more intense than in others, but I have not found any family where the flame is not burning at all. This is crucial to the main purpose of this research which is to determine whether the Jewish primary school or the children could be a catalyst in re-igniting the 'flame of Jewish identity'.

There were, however, three families who stated that they were unwilling to increase their level of religious observance, even at the request of their children.

Consider the comment of the wife of family (111/99).

> *'In the past I would have gone further. I don't think that I would now. I think that's the situation that we have reached now. So far and no further. But now I think that we've actually reached a point with what we want to do.'*

The husband of family (112/98) was unsure what his future response would be, but felt that he would not, at that moment, consider any request to increase his own level of observance:

> *'Today, if you ask me today, I will say no, there is no chance. If you ask me today I'd say, no sorry. What you see is what you get and what you have.'*

Finally, to end section 1, I quote the wife of family (118/98) who was quite sure of her response even if it resulted in the creation of major problems.

> *'I would cope with it fine, if he didn't impose it on us. If he moved out and lived his own life, that's absolutely fine. Whenever I would want to see him I would fall in with whatever he wanted in his own home. But I would not want him to impose it on us. I would find it a problem. I would try and compromise. If he wasn't willing to*

compromise we would have a big problem. I don't know how we'd solve it but we wouldn't be happy would we? We've found our level I think, I don't know what we'd do. It wouldn't make for easy living. I think that we'd become quite acrimonious, irritated by each other. I don't think that either would give. So I think we'd have problems.'

Section 2: What might have been the level of the religious observance of the parents if their children had not attended a Jewish primary school?

Family (112/98) felt that the impetus for their religious observance had come from the school and would have been greatly reduced had their children attended a non-Jewish school.

'The impetus had to come from somewhere. We didn't choose the Jewish school because we wanted it to have an effect on our lives, but it has. We chose it because of the children. It wasn't any kind of deliberate move.'

Family (124/99) were equally sure that the Jewish school *'had a tremendous influence'* on their own level of religious observance and that they would *'have drifted'* without this influence. It was also the social friendships that were made between parents.

W: *'I think that we'd have drifted actually.'*

H: *'We might have, but then, because of your family there would have been a certain link.'*

W: *'Yes, but not to this extent.'*

H: *'It would have been more of an imposed thing than part of everyday life. I think that's probably what draws you in, it becomes part of your everyday life.'*

W: *'I think that the school had a tremendous influence. That's how I made my friends.'*

Family (133/99) needed the school to back up the religious life of the family. As far as religious observance was concerned, it appeared that the school had taken on the role of being 'significant adults' for their children. The husband still felt however that it was the role of the parents and the home to provide the religious background and ethos. The grandmother of the children was also present at the interview and made a most pertinent observation.

> *'I think that the big difference is in the relationship between children and parents, there's input from both sides. We haven't all got time in our lives to give them all the background that they need.'*

At that point her daughter (the wife of the family) added what I consider to be the central point of all the above comments of this family:

> *'I couldn't give them that choice. I need the school to back me up. We can't all be significant adults for our children and they have to have their significant adults.'*

Family (130/99) realised that they could not offer their children a sound Jewish experience at home and thus relied on the school to instil this. They had no doubt of what would have been the result of not sending them to a Jewish day school.

> W: *'Probably we would have been less religious. I mean we have friends whose children go to non-Jewish schools but they are more religious than we are and the children haven't lost out on anything. One thing I knew that we did worry about. I knew that we were very middle of the road and I wouldn't be able to give them that background if I didn't send them to a Jewish school. I personally couldn't give them everything that they have got from a Jewish school because I'm not so observant.'*

> H: *'I see the school as almost being like a parental substitute in the sense that they do so much for the children in Jewish education. It leaves us with very little that we have to do to teach them. They get it from the school. It's a part of their daily life.'*

The wife of family (114/98) stated that had the children not attended a Jewish school their life would have been different and they probably wouldn't do as many things as they do today.

'Well first of all, they wouldn't go to shul on the festivals they would probably only go to shul on Rosh Hashanah and Yom Kippur. I think I would have done what my parents did. On Sukkot and Shemini Atzeret and the first two days of Pesach we went to shul, but on Pesach I still went to school and things like that. I think that I probably would have still sent them to school. I suppose that it would have been very different. I think that I would have still done the same on Friday night because I think that the tradition at home is very important.'

The husband also considered the other implications for their children due to the absence of a Jewish day school education.

'I think that here would have been big differences. As a mother and father we would be very concerned if they weren't at a Jewish school in terms of having Jewish friends and I think that we would have been looking at after-school clubs and other activities to try and get them involved in the Jewish way of life.'

The wife of family (106/98) felt that the school had given the family a Jewish cultural environment and had the children not attended a Jewish school there was every likelihood that their Jewish life could be forsaken.

'It would have been different. I think I would have either played more of a part in the religion to give her that start or not doing it at all, and forget it. You know, we're just not religious at all.'

She spoke of her brother's family who were totally divorced from a Jewish life.

'They have two children who have no idea that they have anything to do with the Jewish heritage whatsoever. They don't have any religion. They are completely atheist. Had we have not lived here, that would have happened to us I think, not being a part of the Jewish community.'

Family (116/99) felt that Jewish life would be harder without a Jewish school and that *'probably we wouldn't be doing a lot of the things that we are now doing'.* The children would probably remain at school on festivals that fell on a normal weekday and that many other aspects of their Jewish life would lessen and probably end.

> *'From the religious point, probably we wouldn't be doing a lot of the things that we are now doing. If my children were at a non-Jewish school and it was winter, I'm not sure whether I would say that I would go to the different schools and pick them up early. I'd like to think that I would but I don't know. As it is now, I'm all ready for Shabbat when they come home. It might be at Shavuot time or the last two days of Shemini Atzeret, I might think that because school is so important, well these festivals are not that important and they would be easy to give up. They might be missing too much work. So those things start going.'*

The husband of family (108/99) felt that the family currently depended on the Jewish school to give their children a sound Jewish education. Without a Jewish day school it would have been more difficult.

> *'We would have been under pressure to keep their Jewish education going.'*

His wife added:

> *'I personally feel that I would have been a lot less relaxed about Halachic things than I am. I feel that because they go to a Jewish school, to a certain extent I feel that I can relax about certain details.'*

The husband of family (146/99) made a similar comment:

> *'Well I think that in a way it would have made our lives a little more difficult only in the sense that by going to a Jewish school and mixing with Jewish children and being taught about all aspects of being Jewish, it's meant that it's taken the pressure off us to have to do it at home.'*

He added that it would have been necessary to reinforce their child's sense of Jewish identity at home.

'So if he'd have gone to a non-Jewish school it would have put a lot more pressure on us as a family unit to provide time to make sure that he was given the more specific knowledge that I believe is required.'

The wife of family (119/98) was aware of the necessity of a greater and deeper parental stress on Jewish life.

'We would probably have to answer a lot more questions. We would have had more input ourselves. We would have had to have been more religious to show that, especially with the Chaggim, I mean on Pesach that they can see me changing things around. With all the other festivals like Simchat Torah we would have had to have done a little bit more and actually read a bit more about it. And they would have to go to cheder lessons.'

Her husband then added that he was also aware of the implication of the increased number of non-Jewish friends their child would have and the corresponding need for the family to invite some Jewish friends in order to ensure a contact in that respect.

Section 3: Additional comments by parents regarding their anticipated future level of religious observance

All the families who were interviewed were asked about their anticipated future religious observance. These additional responses I have selected below are very similar in content to those of the great majority of the families who saw themselves as continuing to live the way they were at the moment.

'We will probably stay at the same sort of level. I see some sort of initial fluctuation. We might turn on the television on Shabbat or have less religious friends round or visit them. But we would stay generally with the same way of life.' (123/99)

'It's kind of routine now. It is so much a part of our lives that I couldn't ever envisage myself not doing it. So I can't see that we will become any less because this is now what we do. It's not a problem what we do because it's what we've always done.' (107/99)

'I think that where we are now, we will carry on doing it. We will still go to shul on Rosh Hashanah and Pesach. But I don't know if I'd go on Sukkos or Shavuot. I don't know, it depends on as you say it's a "what if" situation. If in ten years' time we got involved with the shul we could end up going even more. You know, you just don't know.' (109/98)

'Our established pattern suits us. We're comfortable with it. This is the lifestyle that we feel comfortable with.' (121/9)

'I think that if it was just me and the wife at the end of the day, our observance within these four walls would probably increase whilst our observance outside of these four walls would probably decrease. But who knows?' (126/99)

Most families felt that there would be no real change in the future to their current level of religious observance. The response, however, of both husband and wife of family (131/99) below when asked this question is worthy of a more detailed analysis. There are so many deep-seated reasons given by this family regarding their anticipated future level of religious observance that it is well to analyse them section by section. As both husband and wife appeared to be at one with each other, the responses are given for the family and not designated husband or wife.

- *'I can't see us or myself being that observant. I enjoy going to shul. Our friends are very similar to us. We haven't moved that far forward that I think that we will move back again. We will probably stay at the same level.'*

- *'I think that I'd probably go to shul a little less than I do now because I go more for the children now.'*

- *'There was a time when I would have liked to become more religious but you can't do everything.'*

116

- *'My husband feels that it's too much sometimes to be that religious. We live in a sort of compromise. Every so often I get a feeling that I would like to be more religious but on the whole I think that we each sort of compromise. It's a big jump to do this when you've been doing what we're doing now and then to become Shomer Shabbat, for me it's like a chasm, I can't really cope with that.'*

- *'I know that we considered it very seriously. But now I realise that it's not practical because I haven't got family like with friends who are interested enough to do this.'*

- *'Other people have a family or circle of friends who are interested enough and they all get together and they are socialising. You have to do that on a Yom Tov or you would go out of your mind with boredom. Unless you have been to shul, that's it. It's a very long day if it's only you and the children and you can't do anything else.'*

- *'I think that we are comfortable the way we are therefore unless we changed but I couldn't see any reason to change.'*

There was a clear indication that this family had no intention of being fully observant in an Orthodox manner. The two main reasons given were firstly that, regardless of any religious activities undertaken for the sake of their children, they did not feel that they had really moved that far forward in a religious sense. Secondly, their own friends were similar to them, so their social life was unlikely to change. Once their children were older they would probably not go to the synagogue quite as frequently. Neither felt that religious life would disappear but that there would have to be a compromise. Once their children were much older and were no longer dependent on their parents to the degree they experienced in earlier years, the parents admitted that they saw little reason to continue leading such a religiously observant life.

Some final thoughts about the parents' anticipated level of religious observance in future years

Although the majority of the families appeared to be prepared to increase their own level of religious observance at the request of their children, each family emphasised that such an increase would be dependent on what was asked of them. In some cases it was clear that there was a difference of attitudes between husband and wife.

When parents were asked what their level of religious observance might have been had their children not attended a Jewish primary school, the responses were very revealing. The great majority of families interviewed clearly indicated that their own current level of religious observance would certainly have been far less had their children not attended a Jewish primary school. There might have been no other incentive for them to lead a more religiously observant lifestyle. This is a very clear indication of the direct effect of the influence of the school on the lives of the parents.

Chapter 10

The final conclusions of this research

The evidence from the analysis of the data of both questionnaires and interviews gives a very clear indication that there has been a noticeable and positive change in the level of religious observance and practice of the majority of less or non-observant parents which directly or indirectly can be attributed to the influence of the children and the school.

In this respect, the data yielded similar results in all three of the schools which participated in my research. This is particularly interesting given that the three were initially selected because of marked differences in the communities they serve, their geographical locations and their specific ethos. I also found no noticeable evidence when looking for any pattern in the increase of levels of observance to suggest that countries of origin of parents and grandparents of the children might have been a contributory positive or negative factor.

It was clear from the data presented that the areas relating to the greatest increases of religious observance were in respect of the Jewish dietary laws and synagogue attendance on Sabbath and festivals, coupled with an increase in the observance of specific commandments and customs relating to the Sabbath and festivals.

The overriding reasons given by parents to send their children to a Jewish day school highlight a desire, regardless of their own level of religious observance, to ensure that their children will retain and maintain a sense of 'Jewish identity'. The choice of a Jewish school was also important to those parents who did not want their children to experience the problem of being a minority group in a larger school.

Parents also expressed their fear of future intermarriage. An assumption might be drawn that, in opting to send their children to a Jewish school, the parents have already made the decision for their children to receive a good foundation of Jewish knowledge and Jewish identity which parents hope will sustain them in later years. At no time did parents say that they expected changes in religious observance in their own lives due to their children attending a Jewish day school.

It was clear that the great majority of parents were delighted with the form of education their children were receiving, which, in frequent cases, they saw as providing a substitute for their own inadequate Jewish knowledge.

In an earlier chapter, I drew attention to several examples of previous studies in the USA which stress the important role of parental support for the religious ethos of the school. This was viewed as a major factor in ensuring their children's future adult identification with Judaism. The main body of evidence in my own research has clearly indicated, however, that by contrast the majority of families who have increased their level of religious observance have been influenced directly or indirectly by their children. It was clear that for these families, their children had become the communicators of Jewish identity and practice.

It is my contention that the conclusion from this research study has brought with it a further crucial implication. The parents who have participated in my own study have indeed shown support for the religious ethos of the school, thereby increasing their own level of religious observance. Such changes in parental religious observance may well increase the likelihood of the adult identification of their children with Judaism.

Through the influence of the school and their children, parents can be brought only to a certain level of observance. At that time they are 'ready' for another external influence to take them to the next stage. This could be due to an observant friend or perhaps attending a school Shabbaton where they meet other observant families who could influence them. Schools could create such further opportunities for the parents.

For the great majority of parents who participated in this study, what had started as a way of doing something for their children has ended with a resurgence of greater family commitment to Jewish identification.

Principally as a result of the existence of Jewish day schools, it appears that many Jewish families are now more positively involved in a more religiously observant life-style.

So where do we go from here?

The Institute for Jewish Policy Research, together with the Board of Deputies of British Jewry, is currently engaged in a thorough and comprehensive survey of the Jewish community in the United Kingdom. The results of that survey will give community leaders some indication of current trends in communal needs and demography. The IJPR has also published *The Future of Jewish Schooling in the United Kingdom* (Valins, Kosmin and Goldberg 2001) which documents the growth and potential of existing and new Jewish schools. London and Manchester remain as the main centres of growth and stability whereas other provincial Jewish communities appear to be shrinking in number because of the younger generation moving away to join the larger Jewish communities in other areas or going on Aliyah to live in Israel.

During the last ten years there has been a rapid expansion of Jewish day schools in London, both primary and secondary, catering for pupils both from the Central Orthodox and the Progressive communities. There is also a growth in the number of schools for the more right-wing ultra-Orthodox communities.

The great majority of parents in my own research study, regardless of their own current level of religious observance, have stressed that they wish to support the values and ethos of the Jewish day school attended by their children. The old established JFS (Jews' Free School) has moved to purpose built premises in North West London. With a ten-form entry it will remain the largest Jewish secondary school in Europe. Another large Orthodox Jewish secondary school, Yavneh College, has now opened in Elstree. There are also plans to open a further Jewish secondary school in North London which will cater mainly for the Reform/Liberal community but which will be available for all segments of the Anglo-Jewish community.

Within this communal agenda, my research is able to offer clear evidence of the extent to which parents have been affected and influenced directly and indirectly by the school and by their children as pupils of the school. In the light of this evidence, schools may wish to consider the results of this research study and its implications for Jewish identification of pupils currently attending Jewish schools. In order to maximise the effects and influence of Jewish day schools, the schools might be interested in taking note of the following four areas highlighted by my own research:

[1] The results and conclusions of this research study which have shown that parents of pupils at Jewish primary schools in England can be influenced directly by their children and indirectly by the school, resulting in an increase in their own level of religious observance.

[2] The results and conclusions of my research study which have indicated the main expectations of parents who chose a Jewish primary school for their children. These expectations can best be divided into six groups which are set out below.

- Ensuring that their children will retain and maintain a sense of 'Jewish identity'. As a minority group in a multicultural society, Jews are no different to other groups who strive to determine their own individual and group identity. This is certainly an area for future research.

- Developing a love and pride of being Jewish.

- Providing a sound Jewish education either as a substitute for the parents' inadequate Jewish knowledge or to reflect the earlier Jewish education of the parents.

- Providing a warm and happy Jewish family atmosphere and environment.

- Benefiting from the communal aspects of the school which act as a catalyst and focal point for increased parental and family contact with other Jewish families in the community.

- Benefiting from the combination of secular/Jewish education during the school day.

[3] The importance of the following aspects of school–home relationships:

- the impact of vibrant Jewish education on home activities

- the role and importance of parental education

- the coherence of Jewish parents' understandings and commitments in line with those adopted by Jewish day schools.

[4] The importance of previous longitudinal research carried out in the USA which has shown that only when parents have supported the religious ethos of the Jewish school will the pupils continue to identify with Judaism in later years. There is no reason to assume that this will not also be the case in UK Jewish schools.

This study has demonstrated that if parents are satisfied with the education and ethos of the school and are aware that their children are happy and benefiting from the education provided, they will be more receptive to the religious activities and influence of the children. In short, this research has highlighted the main factor which has been a major influence on the religious attitude and practice of the parents and which has influenced them to increase their own level of religious observance, namely the religious activities of the children and comments made by the children at home. In a practical manner this implies that Governors, headteachers and heads of Jewish Studies of Jewish primary schools should give attention to those areas of the Jewish education curriculum which the pupils can bring back to their own homes.

Evidence from this study has shown that children bring home the enthusiasm and excitement of demonstrating their skills at singing songs of religious significance such as the Grace after Meals, introducing songs and stories into the Pesach seder service and involving the family with the joyous festivities of Purim and Chanukah. When the children encourage their parents to take them to the synagogue on Sabbath or festivals it is often the result of the interest of the children caused through similar events simulated at school.

Evidence has also been found to indicate the willingness of parents to want to learn more because of the example brought by their children. This was frequently coupled with their feelings of inadequacy arising from their own poor and more limited religious education.

It follows then that Jewish schools must continuously strive to excite and encourage their pupils in such a way that they will want to introduce the experience to their own families. When children grow up within a family that supports the religious ethos of the school, and who have become familiar with some or all of the Jewish rituals and customs, there is a far greater chance that they will continue to identify as Jews in adult years.

In conclusion, Jewish day schools should seek to ensure a happy and healthy link between their aims, the Jewish Studies curriculum and the aspirations of parents. This research has presented comprehensive data about the background and current levels of Jewish identification of 234 families and their attitudes to their children's schooling.

Although this research has shown that levels of observance have changed positively among the majority of these parents, we need to know whether such changes will have any long-term impact on the future Jewish religious identification of their children when they become adult. This enquiry could be the subject of future research.

A final statement

In his assessment of the current situation regarding Jewish identity, *Will We Have Jewish Grandchildren?*, Chief Rabbi Sir Jonathan Sacks paints a potentially gloomy but realistic picture for the future. I hope that the conclusions I have reached in this research study will give a more positive message of hope and encouragement to those planning and building and maintaining Jewish day schools in the UK.

A fellow researcher in the USA (Rosenblatt 1999) stated that: 'we might be witnessing a reversal in the direction of transmission' where the children have become the teachers of their parents. The evidence of my own research study appears to support this concept, which has also been recorded in the words of the Biblical prophet Malachi some 2,500 years ago:

> *'He shall turn the heart of the fathers to the children, and the heart of the children to their fathers.'*

Bibliography

A brief message to the reader

This book focuses specifically on the main findings of my doctoral thesis. The comprehensive bibliography listed below contains all the sources I consulted when undertaking primary research on the effects of Jewish primary schools on less or non-observant families. Although the majority of these are not mentioned or included in this book, they are all superb contributions to the subject and worthy of further study.

Becher, H., Waterman, S., Kosmin, B. and Thomson, K. (2002) Planning for Jewish Communities. A Portrait of London and the South-East: A Community Study. London, Institute for Jewish Policy Research.

Board of Deputies of British Jews (1999) Community Research Unit survey: Attendance at Jewish Day Schools.

Bock, G.E. (1976) 'The Jewish schooling of American Jews – a study of non-cognitive educational effects', doctoral thesis, University of Harvard.

Cesarani, D. (ed.) (1990) The Making of Modern Anglo-Jewry. Oxford, Blackwell.

Cohen, S.M. (1974) 'The impact of Jewish education on religious identification and practice', Jewish Sociological Studies, Vol. 36, pp. 316–26.

Cohen, S.M. (1992) 'What we know about the marginally affiliated', in S.L. Kelman (ed.), What We Know About Jewish Education. Los Angeles, Torah Aura Productions.

Cohen, S.M. (1997) 'Day school parents in conservative synagogues', in J. Wertheimer (ed.), Jewish Identity and Religious Commitment: The North American Study of Conservative Synagogues and Their Members. New York, The Jewish Theological Seminary of America.

Cooper, H. and Morrison, P. (1991) A Sense of Belonging: Dilemmas of British Jewish Identity. London, Weidenfeld & Nicolson.

Dashefsky, A. (1992) 'The effects of Jewish education on Jewish identification', in S.L. Kelman (ed.), What We Know About Jewish Education. Los Angeles, Torah Aura Productions.

Dashefsky, A. and Levine, I.M. (1983) 'The Jewish family: continuity and change', in W. D'Antonio and J. Aldous (eds), Families and Religions. Beverley Hills, Calif., Sage.

Dashefsky, A. and Shapiro, H. (1974) Ethnic Identification among American Jews. Lexington, Mass., Lexington Books.

Drewinko, A.P. (1999) 'Culturally situated education: parental perspectives on the Jewish day school', doctoral dissertation, Ann Arbor, MI, UMI, University of Indiana.

Encyclopaedia Judaica (1971) Family, Vol. 6. Jerusalem, Keter Publishing House, pp. 1164–72.

Englander, D. (1994) A Documentary History of Jewish Immigrants in Britain 1840–1920. Leicester, Leicester University Press.

Foddy, W. (1993) Constructing Questions for Interviews and Questionnaires: Theory and Practice in Social Research. Cambridge, Cambridge University Press.

Frank (1962) cited in Sanua, V.D. (1964) 'The relationship between Jewish education and Jewish identification', Jewish Education, Vol. 35, pp. 37–50.

Fried (1973) cited in Kelman, S.L. (1978) Why Parents Send Their Children to Non-Orthodox Jewish Day Schools. Los Angeles, Calif., University of Southern California.

Fuchs, J.L. (1978) 'Relationship of Jewish day school education to student self-concepts and Jewish identity', dissertation for degree of Doctor of Education, University of California.

Gartner, L.P. (1973) The Jewish Immigrant in England, 1870–1914. London, Simon Publications.

Goldberg, J. and Kosmin, B.A. (1997) The Social Attitudes of Unmarried Young Jews in Contemporary Britain, Report No. 4, June. London, Institute for Jewish Policy Research.

Goldlust, J. (1970) 'A study of Jewish adolescents in Australia', Jewish Education, Vol. 40, pp. 49–59.

Himmelfarb, H.S. (1974) 'The impact of religious schooling – the effects of Jewish education upon adult religious involvement', unpublished PhD thesis, University of Chicago.

Himmelfarb, H.S. (1977) 'The interaction effects of parents, spouse and schooling: comparing the impact of Jewish and Catholic schools', The Sociological Quarterly, Vol. 18 (Autumn), pp. 464–77.

Ingall, C.K. (1993) 'Soul turning: parent education in a conservative Jewish day school', Conservative Judaism, Vol. XLV, No. 4 (Summer), pp. 50–65.

Jakobovits, Chief Rabbi Dr Immanuel (1971) Let My People Know. London, The Jewish Educational Development Trust.

Jewish Chronicle, weekly publication: Archives from 1845, London.

Kelman, S.L. (1978) 'Motivations and goals: why parents send their children to non-orthodox Jewish day schools', doctoral dissertation, Los Angeles, University of Southern California.

Kosmin, B. (2003) 'A new Jewish secondary school', published as an article in the Jewish Chronicle of 7 November. London, Jewish Chronicle Publications.

Kosmin, B.A. and Levy, C. (1983) Jewish Identity in an Anglo-Jewish Community: The Findings of the 1978 Redbridge Jewish Survey. London, Research Unit of the Board of Deputies of British Jews.

Kosmin, B., Goldstein, S., Waksberg, J., Lerer, N., Keysar, A. and Scheckner, J. (1991) Highlights of the CIF 1990 National Jewish Population Survey. New York, Council of Jewish Federations.

Levy, Rev. S. (1911) Paper presented to the Conference of Anglo-Jewish Ministers. Reprinted in The Jewish Annual for 5704 (1943–44). Cited in Lipman (1954).

Lipman, V.D. (1954) Social History of the Jews in England 1850–1950. London, Watts & Co.

Livshin, R. (1990) 'The acculturation of the children of immigrant Jews in Manchester 1890–1930', in D. Cesarani (ed.), The Making of Modern Anglo-Jewry. Oxford, Blackwell.

Miller, S. (1988) 'The impact of Jewish education on the religious behaviour and attitudes of British secondary school pupils', Studies in Jewish Education, Vol. 1, pp. 150–65. Hebrew University, Jerusalem, The Melton Centre for Jewish Education in the Diaspora.

Miller, S., Schmool, M. and Lerman, A. (1996) Social and Political Attitudes of British Jews. London, Institute for Jewish Policy Research.

Neuberger, J. (1995) On Being Jewish. London, Heinemann.

Neusner, J. (1995) Judaism in Modern Times. Oxford, Blackwell.

Nulman, L. (1955) 'The reactions of parents to a Jewish all-day school', doctoral dissertation, Ann Arbor, MI, University of Pittsburgh.

Pinkenson, R.S. (1987) 'The impact of the Jewish day care experience on parental Jewish identity', unpublished doctoral dissertation, Temple University, Philadelphia.

Ravid, R. (1993) The Relationship between Jewish Early Childhood Education and Family Jewish Practices. Chicago, Board of Jewish Education of Metropolitan Chicago.

Rosen, B.C. (1969) Adolescence and Religion: The Jewish Teenager in American Society. New York, Shenkman.

Rosenblatt, S.M. (1999) 'And you shall teach your children: an exploratory study of the Jewish experience of families with children in Jewish day school kindergartens', doctoral dissertation, University of California.

Russell, C. and Lewis, H.S. (1900) The Jew in London: A Study of Racial Character and Present-day Conditions. Cited by Gartner (1960) The Jewish Immigrant in England, 1870–1914. London, Simon Publications.

Sacks, J. (1993) One People? Tradition, Modernity and Jewish Unity. London, The Littman Library of Jewish Civilisation.

Sacks, J. (1994) Will We Have Jewish Grandchildren? Jewish Continuity and How to Achieve It. England, Vallentine Mitchell.

Sanua, V.D. (1964) 'The relationship between Jewish education and Jewish identification', Jewish Education, Vol. 35, pp. 37–50.

Shapiro, C. (1963) 'An appraisal of current Jewish communal needs', presented at the annual conference of the National Association of Jewish Centre Workers, Cleveland, Ohio.

Shapiro, Z. (1988) 'From generation to generation: does Jewish schooling affect Jewish identification?', doctoral dissertation, University of California.

Sharot, S. (1974) 'Native Jewry and the religious anglicization of immigrants in London 1890–1905', The Jewish Journal of Sociology, Vol. 16, No. 1 (June).

Shindler, J. (1993) 'Marriage trends in Anglo-Jewry: "Where do we go from here?"', Le'ela, Vol. 35, p. 19. London, Jews' College.

Sigal, J., August, D. and Beltempo, J. (1981) 'Impact of Jewish education on Jewish identification in a group of adolescents', Jewish Social Studies, Vol. 44, pp. 229–35.

Valins, O. and Kosmin, B. (2003) The Jewish Day School Marketplace: The Attitudes of Jewish Parents in Greater London and the South-East Towards Formal Education. London, Institute for Jewish Policy Research.

Valins, O., Kosmin, B. and Goldberg, J. (2001) The Future of Jewish Schooling in the United Kingdom. London, Institute for Jewish Policy Research.

Zaiman, H.Z. (1972) 'An approach to Jewish parent education', Jewish Education, Vol. 41, No. 3 (Spring), p. 18. Cited in Ingall (1993).

Glossary of Hebrew words

Aish: A Jewish youth educational organisation

Alef Bais/Alef Bet: The name of the Hebrew alphabet

Aliyah: Emigrating to live in Israel/Reciting blessings on the Torah

Ashkenaz/Ashkenazi/Ashkenazim: Refers in modern-day terminology to Jews whose families lived (or still live) in Central and Eastern Europe

Avelut: Period of mourning

Bar Mitzvah: Confirmation ceremony when a Jewish boy reaches the age of 13

Bat Mitzvah/Bat Chayil: Confirmation ceremony when a Jewish girl reaches the age of 12

Bench/benching: Reciting Grace after Meals (Yiddish name)

Beth Din: The Jewish Court of Law

Birkat HaMazon: Grace after Meals (Hebrew name)

Bnei Akiva: The name of a Jewish youth group

Bracha/brachot: Blessing/blessings

Brit Milah: Circumcision (see also Mohel)

Chag/Chaggim: Jewish festivals (also called Yom Tov)

Challah/challot (pl.): Plaited loaves of bread used on Shabbat

Chametz: Food containing forbidden ingredients during Passover

Chanukah/Hanukah: The Festival of Lights commemorating the rededication of the Temple in Jerusalem during the time of the Maccabees, 2nd century BCE

Chanukiah: An eight-branched candelabra used at Chanukah (see also menorah)

Cheder: Part-time religion classes, i.e. Sunday School (see also Talmud Torah)

Chumash: A book containing the five books of Moses

Chutzpa: Cheek/rudeness

Daven/davening: Praying

Erev Yom Tov: The day before a festival

Etrog: A citron used on the Festival of Tabernacles

Frum: Very observant Orthodox Jews

Glatt kosher: Food which is checked to an even higher degree than normal to ensure that it is 100% kosher

Haftorah: Section of the books of the Prophets read in the synagogue

Haggadah: Book used for the Passover Seder service

Halachah: Jewish law

Hallel: Psalms of praise to God

Hamotzie: The blessing over bread said before a meal

Havdalah: Ceremony/ritual to mark the end of the Sabbath

Hechsher: A rabbinical certificate confirming that food is kosher

Heimisheh: A traditionally Jewish atmosphere

Ivrit: The Modern Hebrew language

Kaddish: A prayer recited by a mourner

Kapporet: A ritual of atonement before Yom Kippur using a live chicken or money that will be sent to charity

Kashrut: Jewish dietary laws

Kiddush: Prayer recited over wine on the Sabbath and festivals

Kippa (sing.)/kippot (pl.): Skull cap(s)

Kittel: A white robe worn in the synagogue on the High Holydays

Kosher: Permitted food

Kvell: Take pleasure in something (e.g. children)

Lag B'Omer: 33rd Day of the Omer – a day of rejoicing due to the end of a plague in Israel, during which thousands of Jews had died during the 2nd century CE

Lubavitch: A Chassidic group of Orthodox Jews

Lulav: A palm branch used on the Festival of Tabernacles

Macher: Someone who likes to get involved in organising things

Maftir: Final section of the weekly portion of the reading of the five books of Moses

Ma nishtana: The four questions at the Passover Seder asked by the youngest person present

Massorti: An Orthodox synagogue run on modern rather than traditional lines

Matzah: Unleavened bread eaten during Passover

Megillah: The story of Queen Esther of Persia told on the Festival of Purim

Menorah: A candelabra used at Chanukah (see above)

Mezuzah: A small case containing part of the Torah written on parchment and fixed on to the doorposts of Jewish homes

Mikvah: A ritual bath

Minhag: A Jewish custom or tradition rather than a commandment

Minyan: A quorum of ten male Jews over the age of 13 required in order for communal prayer to be held

Mitzvah/mitzvoth: Commandment(s) in the Torah

Mohel: A man who carries out the ritual of circumcision (see also Brit Milah)

Omer: Name given to the counting of the days between Passover and Pentecost

Parasha/parsha: The portion of the Torah read each week in the synagogue

Pesach: Hebrew word for Festival of Passover

Purim: A happy festival when the Book of Esther is read in the synagogue

Rosh Chodesh: The first day of the new month

Rosh Hashanah: The Jewish New Year

Seder: Passover festive home meal and prayers

Sedra: The weekly portion of the five books of Moses read every Sabbath

Seed: Adult learning class

Sephard/Sepahrdi/Sephardim: Refers to Jews who families lived (or still live) in either Spain/Portugal or in any of the Middle Eastern countries such as Iraq, Iran, Morocco etc. The population in Modern Israel has both Ashkenaz and Sephard Jews

Seudat sheishit: The third meal on a Sabbath

Shabbat/Shabbos: Sabbath

Shabbaton: An Shabbat experience for adults and children, often residential

Shalom: Peace. Also used as a form of greeting one another

Shavuot: Festival of Pentecost

Sheloshim: Period of 30 days of mourning for a parent

Shemini Atzeret: The extra festival at the end of Tabernacles

Shidduch: An arranged marriage

Shiva: Period of mourning for seven days

Shomer Shabbat: a person who observes the Shabbat

Shul: Synagogue

Siddur: A prayer book

Simchat/Simchas Torah: A festival to celebrate the conclusion of the weekly Shabbat reading of the five books of the Torah and its recommencement

Sukkah: A temporary booth used during the Festival of Tabernacles

Sukkot: Festival of Tabernacles

Tallit: A shawl with fringes (tsitsit) worn by men during prayer

Talmud Torah: Part-time religion classes/Sunday School (see also cheder)

Tefillah: Prayer

Tefillin: Phylacteries, small leather boxes containing parts of the Torah which are fixed with straps to the head and arm of observant Jews during prayers every weekday morning but not on Sabbath or festivals

The Three Weeks: A sad period from 17 Tammuz to 9 Av (during July/August) relating to events dealing with the destruction of the Temple. No marriages are allowed during this period

Tisha B'Av: The Fast Day of the 9th day of the Jewish month of Av which commemorates the destruction of the Temple in Jerusalem

Torah: The five books of Moses

Treife: Non-kosher meat

Tsitsit: An undergarment with fringes worn by Jewish boys and men

Tu Bishvat: The Jewish New Year for Trees

Yeshiva: Adult Learning Academy

Yiddish: A language originally from Europe, spoken by Orthodox Jews

Yiddishkeit: A term denoting a full Jewish life

Yom Ha-Atzmaut: The State of Israel's Independence Day

Yom Kippur: The Day of Atonement

Yom Tov: Collective name for a Jewish festival (see also Chaggim above)

Zemirot: Songs of praise to God sung at the Sabbath table

Index